Trials, Triumphs and Travelling

Motorcycle Chronicals, Volume 2

CJ McLeod

Published by CC Readers, 2024.

TRIALS, TRIUMPHS AND TRAVELLING

First edition. July 2, 2024.

Copyright © 2024 CJ McLeod.

ISBN: 979-8224800711

Written by CJ McLeod.

This book is dedicated to my two sons, **Edward and Martin** who I am proud to say I both like and love them totally.I hope they don't squirm too much when they realise my antics before they were even thought of.

Chapter 1 Triumphs

Growing up in rural Norfolk, England, during the 1970s life was fun and optimistic – the dark post war years were well behind us, and the youth of the day had more freedom and a bit more money in their pockets than in any period of living memory. There were a lot of good times for most of us, and the world was open and full of opportunities and optimism for the future. Politics and serious stuff was for the 'oldies' and most of us did not really think beyond what we were doing for the week. We lived for the 'weekend' and we would scan the local newspaper for the What's On column. There was nearly always a good choice, whether we wanted to see a live band or just a disco in a local pub.

It was generally a good time to be young, the parents had grown up in a time of relative peace and relief after the second world war, with the rationing and national conscription a thing of the past. Most of the parental generation had been part of the 1950s era of rock and roll, with motorcycling or car owning being within the grasp of those with a bit of get up and go. Those parents had then lived through the swinging sixties and seen, or been a part of all the hippy sets and various young groups having their bank holiday battles in the various coastal towns around the country, student protests were rife in the 1960s and the voices of the young had been acknowledged even if not understood by the 'oldies'. There was a bit more tolerance than in their day, and with the contraceptive pill more easily available, sexuality was more open and not as frowned upon as it had been only a decade previously. We did not quite have it all, but we had a lot.

In the mid-1970s I had been dating my boyfriend for about 10 months and we were having a wonderful carefree time, going to the dances at weekends, and during the daytimes there was always something to do. We had just had our first holiday together, going to the Isle of Man with a group of mates; there was so much to do on the island, not just the racing which was exhilarating in itself, but the sightseeing and the total acceptance of the islanders for all the invading motorcyclists. During that time in England it was not uncommon to go to a pub and be faced with a sign banning various sectors of the population, bikers being one of the popular exclusion groups. We were often labelled as anti-social even though most of us were hard working and had earned our bikes – many being used for commuting to and from work. The 'bad boy image' really seemed unfair to me as I felt that in reality it demonstrated that we had a work ethic as opposed to being 'greasy lay-a-bouts' which was a common label given to us. The term Greasers was coined from this perception – and was indicative of the greased back Teddy Boy hairdos (usually with quiff) brought about by applying oils or creams to comb and style their hair as was popular. It amused me that many of the lads spent more time on combing their hair than I did, but as I had waist length hair all I had to do was trap it inside my jacket – job done.

There are so many forms of prejudice in life, and it is universal for people to disregard those who do not conform to their own set of rules without looking to see the facts of the cases. Discrimination is rife and is universal, not limited to one or other group, but really shows the limits of the persons doing the discrimination as it all comes from ignorance and being unprepared to be educated. Personally I find I am never keen on religion either as it seems to me that many people use religion as a weapon. When I look at the world all I see is wars started by religions – perpetrated by people who expect everyone else to see things their way – not being prepared to look at other points of view. I like to think of myself as being an individualist and try to treat others in the way I like to be treated, or put another way, I treat others as they treat me. Mutual respect never hurts. How do you know anything about anyone different to yourself if you never ask them what their point of view is?

Anyway, I digress, so back to my story. Stu and I were enjoying ourselves out and about in our county, and through our many activities we regularly met up with different groups of bikers. There were one or two bike clubs in the nearby towns, and we joined a couple of different groups. We joined the Triumph Owners Group and then the Norton Owners Group as they promised to give discounts at various bike shops, and a discount is always appreciated, especially when one does one's own maintenance. The other one was locally more active and through them we ended up volunteering at various race tracks. As volunteers we marshalled at several events through our involvement with a Norwich Motorcycle Club. One of the most interesting weekends was for a National 24 hour endurance test where we were stationed at the City end of Hall Road in Norwich. We provided proof of riders attending the waystation by way of stamping their road trial log books, and giving out hot drinks, snacks and any other assistance which the competitors needed if we were able to help. It was quite exciting to do the midnight stint, and was an extraordinary thing to be involved with. I was intrigued as to why someone would want to ride for 24 hours, just for the sake of it. Still, many of the people were very interesting and came from all walks of life, this endurance ride providing stories a plenty to tell their mates back in their hometowns. As with any hobby, people go to all sorts of events within their interest just to know they have done it, the bragging rights are proudly displayed in various metal badges or cloth badges attached either on the leathers or cut down waistcoats worn. Motorcycling seemed to attract characters, not just people, the commonality of a motorbike brought us together and seemed to transcend boundaries – the mutual interest overcoming possible fear of the unknowns. If they rode two wheels, we were as one and the roadcraft needed to survive on the highway brought tales of harem scarem to be shared while having a pitstop, usually involving a burger van in a layby. We already knew they were our kind of people, all we had to do was start talking about makes and models and lifelong friendships were made. Strangers were just friends you hadn't met beforehand.

As time went on, Stu and I attended all sorts of motorcycle meetings, and the local scramble track hosted not only scrambles racing, but there were some great Trials events organised in the same area and we went to a few of them too. With so many various forms of competition; road racing; scrambles, trials, endurance and treasure hunts, there was never a dull moment, every weekend gave us a myriad of choice. We did as much of it as we could fit into our precious leisure hours.

It was time for another small holiday, and we chose to go camping for ten days. We headed off to Brands Hatch for a weekend race meet, and although not being involved this time, we happily watched the road racing and our heroes – Peter Williams, Dave Croxford, Mike Hailwood, Agostini, Phil Read, Percy Tait, Paul Smart and many more. We were going to a 400 mile endurance at Thruxton for the following weekend, but circled round the south coast to Fordingbridge to see my nan while we were touring. My nan was a great woman and was pleased to see us. We spent time with her during the daytime while at night we camped at a site just a couple of miles away, near where one of my uncles lived. It was pleasing to know my nan approved of Stu as I had not had any feedback from my immediate family up until that time – mother was not talking to me and I was not welcome at home, my older sister was living abroad still. We spent the middle of the week around the New Forest and were looking forward to the next weekend of racing; we both felt that one long distance race at Thruxton was not to our taste as it was not easy to keep a track of who was where, and on what lap, so could not keep up with who was leading or losing. We found it a bit of a chore but we were glad we had been and experienced it ourselves.

A couple of weeks after our south coast trip the Norwich club were asking for marshals for the main motorcycle racing at Silverstone. This sounded just up our street and our hands reached for the sky without another thought. As marshals we camped at Silverstone for the weekend and were allowed access to the pits area which we took full advantage of. The evenings meant Stu was as usual getting stuck in, helping out with an extra pair of hands for a team doing some of their race prep, while I wandered off to have a peep at a couple of the other race team sections. During my own tour, in a very skimpy top, a pair of hot-pants and black knee high boots, I found myself chatting to two of my favorite riders of the time; Giacomo Agostini and Jonny Cecotto – together with Barry Sheene. Barry had never been one of my idols, but Ago and Jonny Cecotto were. I was in heaven, especially as I spoke fluent Spanish and was able to converse with them comfortably as Ago's Italian shared many similarities to my Spanish and Jonny was from Spanish speaking south America. They were very complementary and we had a great time, laughing, flirting and chatting about all and nothing in particular. Barry was not too happy as he did not speak anything other than English at that time and couldn't keep up with the banter, and I am sure that Ago and Cecotto were both teasing him for fun as I was obviously not interested in him. Ago was another matter, and I would have happily run off with him if I'd been given the chance. A great man both on and off the track, oozing charm and masculinity – he was eye-candy personified. Life was full of promise and I was enjoying myself – thoroughly – with no major worries or cares.

Anyways, my moment of triumph was not to be and my time was cut off when Stu came along and dragged me back to our mates back at camp. Oh well! I'm sure my life could have taken a different tack at that point, but I was thwarted and brought back down to earth, back to normality and the thought that on Monday work had to be endured to provide the money for fun so life went on. We did our stint beside the race track, but being stationed on an inside bend, we were not called on for any emergencies, except we had a bird's eye view of Barry Sheene slapping his tank and retiring from the main race. Couldn't reason why as up to that point his bike had sounded as though it was right on song to me, but Barry wasn't as quick as Cecotto or Ago so perhaps that was it.

Chapter 2 Sofa Surfing - Survival

My mother and stepfather were having troubles – big troubles. My stepfather was having a hard time health wise, and mother was not really conducive to being a caring wife. Caring was not really in her nature whether to the children she bore, or the men in her life. She was a difficult and quite selfish person, and nothing mattered to her except her own belief of what she was entitled to. She had to be the centre of attention, and was not one to shy away from a drink or ten. True to form she often kicked off, and after one particularly bad argument with her I was unceremoniously kicked out, late on a Sunday evening. I went around to a friend's house where they kindly gave me the sofa for the night, but on the understanding that I would have to find somewhere else to go if I could not go home the next day.

Mother was adamant, I was truly out on my ear, she neither cared nor was worried about my fate. For the next few weeks I sofa hopped, and the constant worry of where to live was not conducive to reliability at work as I needed time off work while trying to find somewhere to live. Luckily there was always factory work and it was a worker's market, so I was able to flit from one job to another without much trouble. I also did a few stints working in cafés and restaurants around the coastal towns and managed to survive. I took jobs wherever there was something to do, and I kept my head above water.

Eventually Stu's parents allowed me to stay at theirs, but it was a small cottage, and again the only sleeping available to me to use was on their sofa. However, I was extremely grateful for that and Stu's mum was great – as a mother figure she taught me a lot about running a home, cooking, shopping – we had a good time together as she had two sons, and a bit of a stickler for a husband, Pam enjoyed having a bit of female company in the house. She was a lovely open hearted woman, but a thrifty Yorkshire lass too. Our Saturday morning routine (while Stu was working) was to go shopping in Norwich in her Mini. She often forgot where we were parked in the multi-storey, so I developed a self-survival strategy of remembering where we had parked. Even to this day I habitually make a mental note of where I've left my vehicle, and often reminisce about her when I catch myself looking for parking landmarks in the car park. Pam was a character, and chatted nineteen to the dozen like no-one else in my life since. She would talk in a broad Yorkshire accent, so fast it was sometimes difficult to catch up, but such a great person.

Our weekly shopping trips meant us travelling to Norwich, going to at least three supermarkets, keeping a tally of what things cost where. The shopping lists were always listed in three lines under which supermarket they were normally cheaper, with notes of prices during the previous week's shop. This meant that we had at least three trips back to the car to deposit the various purchases. I think this is where I got the habit of using a wheeled shopper as I have never liked carrying things unnecessarily, or it could have been the advert on the telly for the packets of mashed potato – the little robotic aliens watching a film of a woman carrying heavy bags of potatoes, laughing about the arms stretching – then falling about, saying – 'and then they smash them all to bits'. A great advert, and personal for me as I have always liked things with wheels on so the thinking aligned with my views. So many memories flood back as life happens to remind me of the little things which occur during daily life. People may not be immortal, but they live on in these moments, and the smiles when thinking of my old friends and characters are full of special thoughts. I love how you can pick up an item from a shop shelf and get transported back through the years to a funny incident or two and in that moment find yourself laughing with a friend of old, tears in eyes either of laughter or sadness that the person is no longer here.

Pam was a good friend, but not that great a driver, and we had several hilarious moments. Near misses were a normal occurrence, and she took frequent advantage of having a mechanic for a son. One day she came home quite disheveled, and no car. Her handbag had fallen off the passenger seat and instinctively she had reached down to pick it up. As she did so, she not only took her eyes off the road, but her right hand drew the steering wheel down and she did a right hand turn on a straight road (luckily a rural road) and drove into the gable end of a house about 25 yards off the road. The house stood up well and was more or less undamaged, but the poor mini didn't fare so well. Stu had to retrieve it with the breakdown lorry from work, and spent the next few evenings and a couple of weekends putting it right again. I did go to give him a hand as I was interested in how jacks were used to help pull some bits out, other bits were cut out and replaced or welded, and then watching how Stu resprayed it. He did an amazing job and Pam got on with things as if the event had never happened. She was the best mentor ever to show me how, when life seemed bad, just shrug your shoulders and move on. Lovely woman, brilliant friend, and fun with a big heart. She taught me that there doesn't have to be an 'age gap' and that you don't necessarily have to grow up, just to be yourself.

Being young and social, music was a big part of our life, but living in the same house meant Stu and I spent hours with our records on – writing out the lyrics to our favourite rock and roll songs – and with the words dutifully followed we spent ages perfecting our singing along techniques. We drove Stu's father mad as we gaily sang to Eddie Cochran, Buddy Holly, Gene Vincent, Billy Fury, Jerry Lee Lewis and Carl Perkins to name just a few. Pam used to join in sometimes and completed the caterwauling. There wasn't room to practice our dancing but we knew the rhythms and by the time we hit the weekend dances we didn't have to think much about our steps as we gaily jiggled and jived the nights away to our hearts content. Most clusters of villages would take it in turns to have dances in village halls or pub back rooms, there was always a choice of where to go, and we took full advantage. With Stu being allowed to use his mother's car (courtesy of his car maintenance abilities), and both of us having motorbikes transport was never a problem. We were there, living it up at every opportunity.

Stu's father couldn't wait to get us out of the door for a bit of peace and quiet, so there was never any problem about how long we were out. Also, although he had been a bit of a morose man and quite argumentative I accidentally found out an hitherto secret of his. He was ticklish. With this knowledge to hand, the next time he became a bit grumpy I got his slippers off and tickled his feet. He was helpless, the more I tickled the more he had to laugh (or grimace) and he had to yield – his power had been drained and I like to think that although he would still grump, he was a lot more docile with us. Pam couldn't help but laugh at seeing her strict husband lying helpless. Throughout it all, they had a 'bickering' type of relationship but they endured life together until nature parted them. I like to think I helped lighten their more stressed moments, and that I helped Pam give as good as she got after Gilly got used to being semi-traumatised by me. All I know is that I was helped enormously by their generosity towards me.

All this having fun meant that it had to be paid for, and although I picked up regular casual work, I needed more permanent employment especially as I had a future to consider. Living in a rural area did not make this easy, having previously lived on the coast where waitressing was more available for a young unskilled person, I had to think about what opportunities were available and practical for me to do. There was a bus service but it was 2 hours between busses to and from the city so commuting was not an easy option, and there were not many waitressing jobs in the area. I was too young to do bar work and the local garage preferred boys to work on the pumps and in their workshops, even though I assured them I was keen it was difficult to be taken seriously. The other trouble was finding a job which paid well, girls were again not very well paid even though rents did not discriminate – just as well I neither smoked nor drank alcohol – life was very much against the females of this era.

The only way to earn more was to get into a factory and if you were good on 'piece work' you could earn better monies. I tried my hand in a few factories during this period, so a bit of shoe factory work was good, electronics factories were also lucrative and best of all – these jobs were all Monday to Friday – yahoo, weekends off as needed. As with any workplace, the older more experienced workers would get frustrated with us youngsters, and trying to make us embarrassed or put us to the blush was a game to them. Some of the older women could be quite hard on us to the point of bullying those who they did not think were the right material for the job. You had to be quite tough to survive – and any sign of weakness was ruthlessly pounced upon. Luckily I had by now grown a thick skin and my ability to turn the tables on an adversary saved me from the worst scenarios, my sense of humour also proved immensely valuable. To make others laugh was a great asset as it made any boring chore bearable. To laugh at oneself was even better, as taking yourself too seriously always opens you up as an easy target.

I took a job in an electronics factory in the city, and was able to commute on my Bantam 175cc and braved both the weather and the sometimes very basic factory women who were not always easy with us young girls. After working for a couple of months in electronics, the factory work ran out and some of the workforce was to be laid off, as I was one of the last in – I was a casualty of the 'last in – first out' ethos – and found myself once again looking for employment.

It was back to scouring the small ads with Pam where, after a few false starts, I managed to get work in a music shop for a while. I really enjoyed this job, playing music while helping people to choose their purchases was cool. However, this was not long lived as the music shop's main purpose was to sell pianos, the emphasis was meant to be on classical and orchestral stuff, and having rock and roll blaring out through the shop was not what the owner thought appropriate. I thought this was unfair as several rock and roll groups included piano instruments in their records. I was told I had to play more 'Mantovani' and other placid classical music which I tried my best to do, but couldn't help putting a bit more cheerful stuff on when the boss was out. The supervisor in the piano section was quite a happy chap and usually let me know when the Boss was on his way so I could put his preferred sound tracks back on. However, this pleasant life was brought to a quick end when the boss arrived back unexpectedly early one day while I was blasting out a bit of rock and roll – this culminated in me being found out as being 'the wrong sort' even though my record sales were good. I was asked to leave and yet again found myself without an income. Disastrous, what was I going to do now? Without work I would not have money to ride my motorbike, this was life-threatening, and needed serious planning.

Chapter 3 Factory Work, mmm Chocolate!

I spoke to Stu's mum for help as I had a great respect for her advice – she was a practical Yorkshire woman with a heart of gold. Although I was contributing towards my keep, I had a lot of thinking to do. Pam was ever practical, and obviously it was getting very cramped in the cottage. Pam encouraged me to think about what I was going to do long term. as there was not really enough room for me, in hindsight it was not ideal for a relatively young relationship either.

After several heart to heart discussions we worked out a plan and looked about for a job preferably with accommodation provided – this seemed a sound solution but the practicality was difficult – most jobs with living-in facilities involved late night and weekend working, but worse still paid very little and the accommodation usually stretched the imagination – shared room being the norm, and there was usually nowhere to put my motorbike either. Big problem for a fun loving socialite. I would now have to look further afield.

Undaunted, I applied for several jobs, and it didn't take long. Although there was no accommodation with it, work was soon offered to me and – even better, transport was conveniently provided – there was a works bus which collected us from the village. The bus was fun and gave me the opportunity to meet some of the older women in the village and a couple of them took me under their wing so they showed me where to go, where to get my overalls and introduced me to the supervisor who took me to the other new girls for our introduction to the company.

The induction to the local chocolate factory covered the inevitable health, hygiene and safety lectures, a bit of first aid, and then a brief history of the company. I could not believe my ears when we were told we were 'allowed' to eat all we wanted on the shop floor. What? I double checked and yes, we were 'allowed' to eat all we wanted while on the shop floor. Not only that, we were to have a break in the morning, at lunchtime, and another break in the afternoon, and were allowed to eat from any of the lines that we passed on the way between the workstation and the canteen. Well, I was in heaven. No more offers needed to be made, it was heard loud and clear. I felt I had won first prize in the raffle. Chocolate. I love chocolate. I am a woman, after all. This was great, and after my first day I was over the moon. Chocolate always wins over apple pie and cream, (this reference is for those of you who read my first book).

From the company's point of view this made perfect sense, the idea was that after the first couple of days most factory hands gorged themselves to the point of not wanting to eat another mouthful of chocolate, ever. Not me. After four weeks of this, I couldn't wait for my breaks to see what was on offer on my way to the canteens, the hardest part was planning the route to make sure I tasted different lines. I was definitely getting my belly's worth on a daily basis. All my friends in the factory couldn't believe I could eat so much and not appear to put on any weight, but so it was. It took a lot of believing that we had the freedom to consume to our heart's content. Of the intake of about 30 who started at the factory alongside me, nearly all of us had eaten ourselves silly and were quickly weaned off the idea. After a couple of days of 'all you could eat', twenty nine of us had eaten all we could. Except one. You've guessed, yes, ME. I loved it, and after four weeks I was still loving it. Chocolate while working – heaven – I went to and from the canteen with my head swiveling eagerly on my neck ensuring I didn't miss any treats. So, with a morning break, lunch time and afternoon break I munched my way through the factory. Even better, on a Friday afternoon we had the factory shop where we could buy 'mishapes and seconds' to take home for the weekend. Bags of goodies I could share with friends too. Luckily at the time I was still dancing through about five evenings a week and my hitherto hollow legs were absorbing the calories quite successfully. Before I managed to totally overload myself my life took a nose-dive again.

The factory work was only ever meant to be a stopgap as it did not solve my lodging needs but I was earning enough to put a bit aside to find a flat or bedsit and with that in mind my life seemed stable enough, but all the best laid plans will go awry – and without any more ado mine fell apart very quickly and without any warning. During the next few weeks several steps in my life-plan started disintegrating, like dominoes standing on end, topple one and then the whole line fall over and make a mess.

Although my own father was no longer alive, he had always talked to me about the armed forces saying that was a great career choice with travel options while being trained for whichever trade one chose. Not only that, the pay was good and accommodation was included. During our planning periods Pam and I thought about this and looked at all three services, air, sea and land. I went to the career offices of all of them and took home brochures to study. I decided that the Navy was my preference – inspired by my half-brother who was in the Navy and dad had been so proud of him I thought he might look down on me and approve; with that in mind I went through all the applications and interviews during the next few months and was scheduled for my final interview session in Ipswich. Obviously, this would impact on my relationship with Stu, even though we had spoken about this, there were some aspects that through the various stages of discussion with the Navy office I was aware that a lot of it would change my life in more ways than had previously occurred to me. Naively I thought things would continue and this was a good solution all round, nothing seemed to be a problem. Even better they had women mechanics so that was my career of choice. It all seemed so perfect.

While talking through the options which seemed to be coming my way, Stu stopped me in my tracks by telling me that all the 'training' periods would mean I was going to have to be 'on base' for long periods, he was not willing to have a long distance romance. He knew I had to get a job and that I had to find somewhere else to live so I didn't immediately catch on. Basically in his view, if I did indeed join up, he could not see us working as a couple any more. It was like a punch in the stomach. I thought our relationship could overcome this but Stu was adamant. I had a lot of thinking to do, and eventually came to the conclusion that we had so much fun together I did not want to break up – so I deliberately flunked my last interview. I had passed all the tests I needed with good grades and scores and it came down to this final interview, with one of the questions being – what do you feel about being told to follow an order? My reply was a cheery, that's okay, so long as I am asked nicely! – obviously that was a wrong answer – and I received a 'thank you for your interest in joining us, but...' letter.

Motto is – always look on the bright side of life – at least I still had my chocolate munching work, and I was earning my keep plus some, and I thought that was the answer to keeping my relationship intact.

I had only been at the chocolate factory for about 10 weeks, when I got a distressed phone call from my stepfather. I came away from that call in turmoil. My life was not my life, it seemed.

Chapter 4 Tribulations (Mother's tricks)

Mother had been having an affair and had left my stepfather for a younger man. Worse than that, my brother was only about five years old and had been left with his dad. This was not good as stepfather had lost one leg the previous year, and his health was still not good as he had taken a further turn for the worse, he had his second leg amputated only a couple of weeks before, mother was not a particularly caring wife at the best of times; he was floundering, helpless and heartbroken. It was almost impossible for him to look after an active and escapologist five year old while he was himself wheelchair bound. On arrival back at the family home, I found that not only was mother nowhere to be seen, my younger sister had already decamped to a friend after her own dispute with mother just weeks earlier. Would I go home permanently and help, as he was out of his depth and not coping very well? I knew this was an impossible plea to refuse, but I rode over to see just how bad things were.

After talking with my stepfather, we decided that I should move back home, give up my job and take over the reins of the household. The responsibilities were a 24/7 commitment so I had to resign from my factory job which I did with a heavy heart. At least now I had somewhere to live with a room of my own, I was already used to looking after my brother and had learned to cook and clean at an early age. I was devastated but knew I had no choice. I went back to Stu's and after a good chat with Stu and his parents explaining the situation, I was unsure if this was the right thing for me, but what else could I do? I packed my stuff up, loaded it all on my little BSA Bantam and returned home.

My stepfather and I went to the bank, stepfather started a new account up and I was given authority to draw on the new account – mother was no longer able to draw out any funds. With access to monies from his bank for housekeeping and a bit of money for myself, it should have worked okay. In fact, with less money going on alcohol we actually started getting on quite well. My brother was at school during the day so I was able to have a bit of downtime but there was no way to get out for a night out. The next couple of weeks were a bit of a blur as I took on responsibility of running the household, but thanks to Pam I now had good economical housekeeping skills. So far, so good. It was a bit strange having to help with the personal care side of things, but we worked out that so long as I helped him into the right place, he could address much of his own very personal bits and bobs. As we say in Norfolk, 'jobs a good'un'.

I was pre-occupied with my new responsibilities and did not see the change in my relationship with Stu, and during a date with Stu he broke off with me. This was a bit of a shock as I thought that we were happy together, but he was unable to fully accept my family problems and I understood that, our family was quite dysfunctional and oddball. Although I had given up my plans for a career in the services to be with him, at least I was able to take on the responsibilities of home life so perhaps that was what was meant to be. We parted amicably but I was devastated, and he promised if I needed help with my bike then I could still call him. I still thought the world of his mother and father too and visited them often when I was in their area.

The positive thing about this period was that I learned more of my stepfather's life than I might have known had I not had to sit with him; we talked more than we had in the seven years he had been with mother. He became more of a person to me than just the other adult in the house. Although I knew he had been one of Denmark's top architects and had come to England to help the UK's transformation with weights and measures working in an office in London – important enough to have a reserved parking spot just inside Marble Arch – other than that I began to see him in a different light.

I became aware he was from a privileged background and some of his childhood exploits amused me. The family had a large farming estate in Denmark where he had an idyllic childhood. His father was a doctor by profession, and his mother had been an Olympic Swimmer in the 1920s. Aged about six his own mother was quite indulgent and occupied with his two siblings so he devised his own games much of the time. One of his early antics had occurred after being taken to an early air show by his father. Armed with his newfound interest at the airshow, he spent a few weeks 'building'. Acquiring various items from around the farmhouse and the farm workshops, with access to books from their private library in the family farmhouse he kept himself amused. With a relaxed parent he contented himself until his mother started noticing things were 'missing' from the house. Her worries seemed inconsequential until she spotted the young boy excitedly running upstairs with an axe in hand. She ran upstairs after him, calling out 'what are you doing?' Her adventurous son called back over his shoulder as he disappeared into the spacious loft – 'come see, mother'. She ascended into the loft to see her offspring's legs disappear up a ladder and out through the loft hatch onto the roof, axe still in hand. She got to the top of the ladder to see the varmint sitting in his homemade wooden airplane – the frame encased in some of her best sheets. It was levitating slightly in the wind, tied to the chimney pot with a bit of rope – she was helpless with only her head above the roofline watching in horror as he swung his axe and chopped the rope. With a whoop of total joy, and oblivious to his mother's fright, he flew about 200 yards over the barn and managed to glide down into the field beyond.

His love of all things mechanical was followed up as soon as he was old enough; he joined a local flying club and became a bone fide pilot. He was eventually very involved in the second world war, becoming a spitfire pilot within the Norwegian Air Force in England and progressed to a prisoner of war when he was shot down during a sortie over Germany. In the German regime he was rebellious and tried several escapes culminating in a few stints in solitary confinement. Finding this out, with the help of a few of his friends we managed to have a couple of trips to a pub at Scottow, near North Walsham where the war hero Douglas Bader was a regular at the time. When he met my stepfather they had several chats about their wartime exploits and incarcerations. The pub had a lot of airplane artefacts around which sparked many a memory for both the veterans, and vastly helped my stepfather to come to terms with his loss of legs, which Doughlas Bader had overcome and never let himself be held back by. I think these trips were helpful, and gave another perspective on life and attitudes. This interlude did not last though and it was not long before everything went upside down again.

Mother! She had gone off our radar, but when she realised she no longer had access to Stepfather's money she arrived home without notice one evening. Stepfather loved her very much, and wanted her back, so it only took a couple of days for me to be pushed out once again. The problem this time – I had nowhere to go and no job. I had many friends so had to sofa surf again. My social circle were really great and I was able to spend several nights here or there, changing venue every two or three nights so that I did not outstay my welcome. This was very much a constant worry, and in the back of my mind at all times. The evenings were mostly spent at the local pubs just to give me something to do, and I was good at networking so my friendship circles grew all the time.

Chapter 5 Not Back Home but Back Out

My life was obviously in a recycle period, mother was back home, so I was back out. I was barely eighteen years old and homeless for the second time in my life. Thankfully I had a social circle and my wits, which somehow helped me to stay relatively sane and to work through my problems as best I could. It helped me to analyse my needs and keep me alive to opportunities. Money, money, money is the first need from which other needs become affordable. So important to be self-sufficient as in the 1970s there was no bank of mum and dad, especially in my case. Mother had the family purse strings back in hand, and my allowance was withdrawn. Thankfully I had saved some of my money from the chocolate factory and my housekeeping for the month I had been back home. Finding somewhere to live was my next problem to be resolved. Work was also a priority so that I did not deplete what monies I had.

After a couple of abortive attempts to get work, I landed a place at a local canning factory. This was an eye opener and the noise was unbelievable. The money was quite good for me and I was grateful for some stability. Plus I liked working in a factory as it was nine to five, Monday to Friday, so weekends were free to have fun. I was on the up again.

The factory floor was astounding, and what hit first was the incredible noise. The empty cans were on conveyors which went overhead to the various lines. They clicked and clacked, thousands of cans tousling along up to twenty metal runways with no sound absorption. I don't know what happens in modern times, but we weren't even supplied with ear plugs. Once the cans were filled with their contents and the lids sealed on, they were slightly quieter as gravity and fillings stilled the echoes in the cans, but they were still noisy. My first job was in the packing area which was in the quieter section as by the time the cans got to the end of the line, they were boxed. We had to label and tape the boxes and then stack them on the pallets, eight boxes of 24 cans per layer, built in a certain way so they kept stable to four boxes high. It was easy work even though physical, and being busy meant the days went quickly.

After working in the packing section for a couple of weeks, I was asked if I wanted to try working on one of the lines. Always up to try my hand at new things I said yes and was taken to the carrot line. This was on a raised framework and the carrots arrived on a central belt left to right transferring onto two separation belts at the end of the first run. These two belts then took the produce back past two lines of operators, right to left. I was quite happy to look and check the quality of the carrots, and put the bad ones onto a small belt going back left to right into the bins. What could go wrong? The next thing I knew I was being carried to sick bay on a stretcher. I had fainted. I couldn't understand what had happened to me, as I could cope with speed, heights, all sorts. Apparently nearly all newbies would faint on the carrots as the colours going three ways in front of our eyes would cause fainting and was a source of amusement for the old hands. We had it tough back then. I gave it another go the next day and was alright then as I knew to look away every so often to stabilize my brain.

I was happy to be earning again, and the only problem was factories start early. I have never been an early bird, night owl was more me, but money being essential I had to cope. The other reason to help me get myself up was that I needed my evenings for social gatherings. So the only time to work is early. Hey ho, off to work I go. With a morning break and lunchtime we were soon homeward bound mid-afternoon. To freedom.

I was commuting about 15 miles to work on my bike and as it was late spring I loved the ride to and from work. Racking up at least 150 miles a week commuting, plus the evening and weekend rides I was quickly becoming an accomplished rider and after my first accident managed to keep upright and in one piece. I loved the freedom of following my own road as it felt like having a horse, without having a need to have a field to keep it in. In my mind I was riding the range like the cowboy my father had been (he will have his own book later). Best of all, although not quite singing and dancing to work, I was able to sing and dance the nights away – that was always my silver lining. So now, the only need still required was where to live.

Whilst grappling with this problem, one evening I went out with a group of friends, I needed to let off steam and the night started out well at the local pub – I was offered the pillion on a motorbike and we were going to go Ten Pin Bowling. There were about a dozen of us in the group and I was to go on the back of Gary for the evening as my Bantam was a bit slow compared to the bikes going for the ride. This sounded good to me, and was an escape from my worries even if it was only for a few hours of fun. It felt good to be in a group of mates with the wind in our hair, and a sporty venue to boot. We had about a 45 mile ride to the bowling alley and it was a good evening. Gary was a relatively new mate and there were a few others I had not met before. We took up about three or four alleys and having bowled before, I was glad to keep my dignity during the evening.

During a loo break one of the other girls was having problems with her chap as she was a bit frightened of him. He was a bit moody and snappy, but I quite liked him as I have always been easy with people who were more difficult characters. The long and the short of this was that we agreed to swap chaps for the rest of the night. We finished our chat and went out to inform our respective rides of the change in partners. Carly was to go on the back of Gary, and I went on the back of Chip. The lads were quite OK with the swap and as we went through Norwich on the way home our friend Jon peeled off with us, the six of us stopped off at Chip's for a cup of coffee. We were chatting for the rest of the evening before heading off home. Gary and Jon took their two pillions home as they all lived close to each other, and Chip was going to take me home in a different direction. We saw the others off first, then decided to have another cup of tea. We chatted some more, and Chip confessed he was not the best company as his previous relationship had ended abruptly and he was concerned that he might have to sell his home – he had based his expenditure on a two income household.

Chip had a two bedroom property and therefore had a spare room. I tentatively probed whether he had thought of renting the spare room out. He had, but was unsure as he was not really a people pleaser, and did not think he would like someone coming in and telling him what to do. I told him my plight, and asked if he would consider renting the spare room to me as I was homeless. I said I was working and prepared to contribute to the household if he would consider me. I said he could take some time to think about it as I didn't want to pressure him if he wasn't keen. However, we talked some more until it was a bit late for me to arrive elsewhere, Chip said I might as well stay the night and we could talk about it the next day. The result of this was I never left, and the last of my problems was resolved, I had somewhere to call home.

Luckily my work was halfway between where I had been living and where I was now going to be based. I still needed to get to work the following week, but Chip took me back to the coast so I could pick up my things and collect my bike. I really enjoyed the ride back to Chip's house, but this was marred by his comment that he hadn't had such a slow ride in years. I was a bit hurt by this as he had a Triumph T150 Trident, and I only had my Bantam which was a sixth of the cc of his machine. Anyway, he wouldn't have to ride with me normally. I would use my own bike to commute, and we were not dependent on each other. However, as our relationship went from strength to strength I would be pillion if we went out socially. No problem.

From a convenient outset, Chip and I got along very well, but there were incidents which meant we had a few rocky moments along the way. We soon became a couple and our friendship developed over the next few months, but we were friends most of all. We would talk a lot, go out a lot, and he had a great caring side to him that not many always saw. One of his best friends had a fatal motorbike crash a couple of years prior to us getting together. David had been an only child and his parents were obviously distraught at his loss. To Chip's credit he would visit the parents every weekend for the next 40 years, and I had every admiration for that loyalty to his friend. There are not many people who demonstrate that sense of closeness for so long. Chip was a funny one, set in his ways quite considerably, but that caring side was genuine.

As we settled into a relatively easy relationship together, we talked about plans and future hopes and he was adamant that he did not want children. This was not important to me either as after being responsible for bringing my young brother up for several years I was glad to be in the same mindset at that time. However, I did realise that I probably liked to think of having my own family sometime in the future, there was plenty of time later in my life. In the meantime I was happy to have the first stable period in my life, work, money and a home without drama.

Chapter 6 Trials

C hip was a British bike enthusiast, through and through. A staunch 'British is best' unionized worker. His father had been a Japanese Prisoner of war and anything Japanese was not considered viable, it was inconceivable for him to have one of those foreign bikes in his garage. He and three of his friends had all bought new Triumph Tridents the previous year and although proud of their bikes, they were all disappointed to have the proverbial oil leaks and other issues with their bikes, Chip's one had an oil leak within the first six months of ownership. He was quite annoyed at the sloppiness of having issues with his brand new bike and it took away his pride in it. The after sales service was not to his satisfaction either and it spoiled his enjoyment. He was particular in keeping it clean and the constant oil leak kept messing it up, annoying him immensely. This was an issue for many bikers who would have been loyal, but found it unsustainable.

I too liked to ride British, but while out shopping in Norwich one day and looking around the motorcycle shops I saw a brand new Kawasaki Z1. I thought it was the best looking bike I had ever come across. There was a 'Bike' magazine with a write up on the Kawasaki, and it had a spectacular centerfold picture of one on a bridge in the dusk, with the streetlights shining on the bike, the photo was stunning and showed the bike off beautifully. I bought the magazine, and after reading the article which was very complementary I left the centerfold open on the coffee table. When Chip got home he saw the photo and read the blurb. He was interested enough to take a trip to Lowestoft the following weekend to see one in the flesh. I was astounded that he was actually impressed enough to look into it. I dare not comment, but was pleased he was looking at them, going so far as to have a trial ride. He did not get the right deal there and then, but a couple of weeks later we went to a dealer in Louth where they took our car in part exchange and we rode home on a lime green Z1. By the time we got home with it, he had bugs in his teeth where he had been grinning from ear to ear. He was hooked. I was astonished that he had actually bought one. The boys were also taken aback as his view on 'foreigners' was bordering on the edge of fanatical at that time. I loved the bike myself, but felt it was too big for me. It did make me want a larger bike than my Bantam though.

It was important to me to be both physically and financially independent, and Chip was happy that I was too as he was very careful financially and ensured we had money between us for necessities. We both had money for personal spending, although he did check to make sure I was not frivolous. One of the first problems we had was when I had passed my motorbike test. I wanted a bigger bike, and he didn't think a girl should have a bigger bike. Out came my defiant streak (or should I say horns). Bowing to Chip's capabilities with bikes, I looked at adverts for bigger bikes, and he came along with me to 'check' they were value for money. It soon became clear that any bike over 250cc was not a good buy. Bikes under 250cc were acceptable. But I had not passed my test to get another small bike, I wanted a bigger one. So, me being me, and not wanting to buy blind, went to a motorbike shop to look at bigger bikes. I soon found a smart 400cc Kawasaki twin. It was ideal and only three years old. I decided to buy it, paid a deposit and set about raising the monies for it. Great. I managed to sell my Bantam quite quickly, and even made a profit of £25.00 over what it had cost me a year or so previously. A bit of my savings and I had my dream secured.

I took a train to Lowestoft to collect my new bike and had a great time, proud as punch as I rode my new steed home – a pretty little Kawasaki Z400, a twin version of the Z1 Chip had just purchased. My confidence ran out as I got home, knowing Chip would not be pleased I hadn't taken him to look it over first, but I was happy. I parked it on the road behind ours and walked home around the corner. It took about two weeks before I had the gall to park it in our driveway. When I did and Chip got home he came in, absolutely furious as he thought I had another man in the house. We had some choice words between us as I told him it was my bike. He was not convinced and ranted for a couple of days until my logbook arrived with my name on it. He was still angry that I had bought it without his approval, but could not deny that he would not have 'allowed' me to buy it. I quietly pointed out that it was not his place to 'allow' me to buy what I wanted with my money. Although he thought I should defer to him, he acknowledged eventually that it was my right to spend my money on what I wanted, and not his decision to tell me. Eventually he gave it the once over, and as it was reminiscent of a Triumph Bonneville in styling, he grudgingly accepted it was actually a smart little bike, and a sensible step up.

With my new to me bike I sought out my younger sister who had also moved to Norwich and I borrowed a helmet to take her for a ride. We had an enjoyable afternoon and I took her home to mine so that she knew where I was living. She met Chip and we had a cup of tea which we carried into the lounge. Chip ended up giggling, and on asking what was so funny, he pointed out we were sitting on the edge of the sofa with our drinks, looking like a pair of budgies on a perch. I guess we were not easy as we had not had much time together for a couple of years and both of us were a bit stilted as we reconnected. I guess it was a bit strange but we relaxed and sat back then. My sister had enjoyed her ride on the back of me, and was happy for me to take her home again. We went back outside, I told Chip I wouldn't be long and off we set. We got about a mile down the road when I got a tap on my shoulder. I pulled over and stopped. In our haste to get going, my sister had forgotten to put her helmet on. I left her at the side of the road while I went back to retrieve the offending helmet. Chip stood there with the helmet which I then carried back to collect and take her home, legally.

I had lots of fun on my Kawasaki and my commute was even more of a joy. I had a top box put on it so that I could use it for shopping and trips to the laundry, happily loading up my workhorse for whichever journey I was on. I would occasionally visit my friends, meeting for lunch and they were often surprised at how 'daring' I appeared to be. Most of them wouldn't dare upset their fathers, boyfriends or husbands by getting their own machine and would laugh at my audacious behaviour. I would just say, 'well, if you know they won't agree, don't ask them, just do it'. I did actually teach a few of my peers to ride, and a few of them did do so, but most of them gave up and stopped riding quite quickly. That was the times we were in, women were supposed to be 'good' so I guess I wasn't. Never mind, that couldn't be helped, I was me and that was that. Although not pleased at first, I think Chip did like the spark I had and my brutally honest assertion that as I was paying for my own life, I could damn well live it.

We did not really ride together very much, but we did plan a couple of breaks. The first one was to have a few days near Brighton, my home town. We would be camping and so it made it easier to take both bikes to get there. I was looking forward to this even though my father had passed away two years before, I wanted to visit his grave, look up some old friends and see a few old haunts, and go to the New Forest to see my nan again towards the end of the week. We were to go on the Saturday so for once I got up early with excitement. I put most of the camping gear on Chips bike, with just my own stuff on my bike. Chip being his inimitable self, decided it would be cheaper to have breakfast before we set off. I said he would have to cook it then, which he did. A full English breakfast – I realised that he had planned this from the beginning as he had all the ingredients ready. Hmmm...

We had breakfast, and of course by then we had to clean up after. I was fretting to go, but Chip had to sort out his tool set to make sure we were prepared in case of emergency. About another hour passed with him tinkering. I was getting a bit wary by then. Of course, it would be daft to not have lunch before we set off. 'if you cook it, I guess'. So, Chip went inside to happily cook lunch. Hmmm. Oh no. I realised there was a football match on the TV. Starting at 3pm – there was no TV at the camp site. Food for thought...

I took my helmet, jacket and gloves outside, he took no notice. I've always thought actions speak louder than words. So, ACTION it was. I wheeled my bike onto the road, donned attire – key in engine and off I went. I had studied the map the night before but already knew where I was headed – I was gone. I had my money for fuel and the week ahead. Although I did not have camping gear, I was good at sofa surfing so I left Chip to his cooking and cleaning and disappeared on my holiday. I did leave a note on his bike saying I was on holiday and would see him next week. I enjoyed my ride to Sussex, found a couple of cafes on the way, and was looking forward to my week. I found out where my father's next door neighbour who had moved to. She was not in, so I had a couple of hours until she was due home. I decided to go to the Palace Pier for a stretch of my legs. I parked up, set off and enjoyed a few ice creams and other niceties available along the beach front. I took my socks and boots off, paddled in the sea and chatted to a few other people on the many benches. I felt really free, had really enjoyed the ease of riding to a place I knew so well.

When I got back to my bike I was surprised to see Chip beside it. Apparently he hadn't realised I had gone until he plated my lunch up and I was nowhere to be found. He eventually went into the garage and saw my note on the seat of his Z1. He couldn't believe I had left him behind, I just said that I thought he had not wanted to have this holiday and that I did. What time did he think he would have set off if I hadn't gone on my own. He didn't really have a good answer so after a warm discussion I followed him to the campsite, helped him unload everything, and said I would be back in a couple of hours after I had caught up with my old friend. Chip's face was a picture as he realised I had not really planned him coming after me. I just said I had not had a chance to see Joan but would be back after I had seen her. I wasn't prepared to argue about it, but I needed a bit of space to decide if I wanted to have him join my holiday. He did learn then that I was not going to apologize for taking things into my own hands, and I made sure he knew I was not going to be a doormat to anybody.

We had a pleasant week away with no more problems. A truce was drawn and we had a good time exploring the coast, seeing some of my old haunts, and ending up at the New Forest before riding home together. Chip did laugh at me, and say he was absolutely gob smacked when he realised I had actually left him at home. He did say that on reflection he should have known I would not give in and that he probably was not really thinking of going camping at all that week. I just said then next time he can book hotels if he didn't want to camp. This amused him as he realised the joke was on him in the end. He was learning not to take me for a fool, although he did try his luck a few times, I guess to make sure of his boundaries. Hey ho.

Chapter 7 Plans and Plotting

Life now was looking more hopeful for the future. For the first time I had a bit of stability and security with a roof over my head, and money in my pocket. There was a routine to our weeks now, not so much dancing during the weekdays but we still met up with mates at the weekends. Fridays started with a ride of 20 miles to the coast where we had a regular meet up with friends in a coastal pub. We would have an hour or so chatting and joking before moving on to another pub chosen by the group. Sometimes we would go bowling, a regular haunt of ours, sometimes we would go meet other friends in another patch of our world. Very occasionally we would go to another friend's house back in Norwich. There was always about ten or so bikes on our rides, lots of banter and chatting. Making plans for the Saturday or Sunday rides. We always had somewhere to go, something to do, whiling away the days in happy camaraderie. Our mates had been friends for several years and most were happy-go-lucky, always up for a laugh or a trip somewhere. If you thought of something to do, it was usually a case of say it and do it.

One evening after a ride out, we gathered back at our place to watch a film and just sit around having a drink or cuppa. That particular evening 'The Italian Job' was on the box and there was about eight or ten of us enjoying this. Seeing the cars careering around Rome, up to their ears in trouble as they frantically drove around fantastic scenic routes was making us envious. One of the group commentated "wish we could ride on those lovely roads". Almost everyone said the same, thinking of riding on beautiful sunlit roads, meandering around awesome bends and it had obviously resonated with all of us present. I piped up with "we can do that! why not do it?"

They all looked at me with one question. How? Having had the experience with my parents when moving from Denmark to Tenerife, I just said that all you do is book the ferries, and ride there. We can get a car ferry from Harwich to Ostend and ride down through Germany to Italy. That let the cat out of the bag.

They asked if I could find out about the ferries and booking accommodation. I said I would get a map of Europe and we could go from there. I would see what ferry companies there were, although I knew that DFDS operated to Europe as my parents went to Denmark that way and I had gone with them. Take a night ferry so we had a fresh start in the morning and off we could go. That seemed simple enough so I was given the task of finding out about tickets etc. We got excited, and agreed to meet the next week to work out who could go, and when was best for everyone to take time off work.

I took to my task with enthusiasm and bought a map of Europe – went into a travel agent to get a book of hotels and motels in Europe, and for information on car ferry services from Harwich. I got a brochure for routes from Harwich and Dover. The brochure of Italian resorts was procured and the information needed was all to hand. The travel agent had never done a self-drive trip, they were only geared up for normal 'package' tours and therefore could not give much more help. But we were going it alone so that was not a problem. I rang up our insurance company to see what we needed to ride on the continent – we needed a 'green card' which they could issue and a 'translation certificate' for our driving licence which they could provide with the green card. They also offered a breakdown service which was recommended that we paid for. I phoned the ferry company for a price and was ready for the weekend get together.

The lads were surprised that it was that easy to organise. Three of us worked in factories and were tied to either the early May holiday or August shut down. We chose the early shut down as we thought that most people who wanted to go abroad would do so during the summer school holidays in August. The travel agent brochure waxed lyrical about several must go to 'monuments and vistas' so we eagerly looked at our map. We were ever the optimists. Holland and Germany would take about a day being only a couple of inches, Switzerland was invisible, and Italy again, we only wanted to go halfway down to the Amalfi coast about another inch or so, again about 12 hours. No problems. We agreed the two weeks was acceptable, I took deposits from the five others who were happy to commit for booking the ferry. I would look for somewhere to stay for our first week in Italy, it was also agreed that it would be nice to spend the second week on the Adriatic coast to visit the San Marino race circuit, so a second stay would be in that region. We could then see Venice on our way home back to the ferry, and being up near the Italian border would be halfway home. All sorted. In our minds we were there.

I researched self-contained places to stay and found a couple of chalets in Sorrento – set in an orange grove – they looked gorgeous and we booked them through the travel agent as they could do that for us, and for the second week an apartment in Rimini near the beach, and only a few miles from San Marino. This was easier than I thought. During our next meeting we all agreed to the grand plan and agreed that the accommodation looked good. We were expecting to have to find somewhere to sleep on the first night, probably somewhere in either South Germany or North Italy and it was decided that as we were not too sure on how easy it would be to find a suitable B&B we ought to take a tent to sleep in beside the bikes. Being roughie toughie bikers how hard would that be for us? Well, we would find out soon enough. For those of you who have travelled over the water, you have the benefit of hindsight from some of us early pioneers, and we didn't. Although we knew at least a few hundred bikers, we didn't know anyone who had toured abroad by then, this was the mid-1970s.

Armed with a full load of ignorance and ambition in equal quantity we blithely looked forward to our trip. Tickets, insurances, driving licence translations, green cards, don't forget passports, chalets and flat booked: the anticipation mounted but we still had packing and emergency camping gear to take. Further meetings and suggestions, tool kits so that between us we could sort problems between us. Tents to sort. How many would be needed, would we need any? Cooking gear? Waterproofs? Again, the innocents abroad played a part here. Thinking B&B rather than camping, Europe has good weather so waterproofs not needed, holiday so no cooking, burger vans will do or cafes will be fine, a tarpaulin hung between bikes would be enough. Yeah, that'll be OK.

Sonny and I both worked at a frozen food factory by then, and we found the perfect solution to the tent problem. Where we worked we used to have to quickly freeze the vegetables when they arrived from the local farms. As they were unloaded onto the conveyors they were swiftly sorted on the lines ready for blanching and freezing. They were then bagged into large 'bins' for storage until they were ready to be packaged. Now what does this have to do with a biker camping session, I hear you wonder? Well, Sonny and I had a Eureka moment around the same time.

Sonny worked on the forklift while I was making up the 'bins'. The 'bins' were huge. They were built around a pallet roughly 5ft by 4ft, We had four posts which fitted on each corner of the pallet, the posts had slots in for the sections to hold the posts in place by metal slats looking like ladder rungs, roughly 18 inches above each other along the sides. We then had cardboard sides to fit within the assembled framework. Voila – we now had a box about 5 foot tall into which we opened and inserted a huge black 'bin' bag. Once the vegetables were put into these huge boxes a cardboard lid was put on top and the boxes were put into the freezers by forklift. At lunch, Sonny and I discussed the bags. Answer to our tent problem? Yeah, easy to pack, unfold and repack after use. Brilliant. We bought a few for our voyage and gaily talked our fellow adventurers into the plan. We could just sleep two to a bag, beside the bikes, no worries. Yes, good idea, sounds the very thing. Camping gear to a minimum. Next...

I was feeling great about the venture, but as usual things do not really ever go straight for me, there was a big fallout just weeks away from our tour. After all the months of excitement life got in my way again. Carly, who was supposedly frightened of Chip. Apparently not so scared that she kept away from him. My friend who I thought was my friend. Apparently she now thought she would like to be his girlfriend, despite knowing full well that we were now a couple. She wanted my man, and my holiday? Where did she get that idea from? This was my stability and security. After what we both had been through I didn't see that coming. But yes. I had been betrayed and let down by someone I thought I could trust and rely on. Double betrayal as it was my stability and someone I thought was my best friend. This all crept up behind me and then spooked me out totally.

Chip had been a saviour to me when I was in a pretty low place and I never gave his loyalty a thought. Our getting together was not inevitable, but we chose each other and had helped each other through a pretty grueling time for both of us. However, this particular day it started out normal, but as I walked into the house after work I just knew something was different. I went through the house and realised straight away that all was not right, it took me about ten minutes to work out what was awry. The bed was made. In our mad morning routine neither of us had time to make the bed, we always left it airing until we got back from work. After remembering his first thought when I had a strange bike outside in the drive was that I was seeing someone, I knew that that must be how his mind works because it is what he would do. Putting the blame on someone for an assumed slight, usually is to deter others from believing you would do that. To be 'outraged' about something usually means they are trying to pretend that is not something they would do. I knew straight away that he was cheating on me. The next few weeks he would start an argument with me and storm out in a rage. It was easy for me to then to go out, and I found out who he was seeing within a week. Carly!

I found them at the pub we used to go to, cuddling up in the alleyway.

I went home, fuming with both of them.

I decided not to confront him straight way, as I would have to find somewhere else to live. But where could I go? It took me a couple of weeks, but I found the absolute right place to move to. I got my things and moved out, but first I stayed home until Chip got home from work. I waited for the inevitable provocation and as he started on I stopped him in his tracks and asked him when he was going to tell me. 'Tell you what,' he said? When was he going to tell me he had found someone else? He then asked me what I meant. I just replied, Carly! He was obviously flustered, but I just said don't worry, she can have you. I'm moving out. He asked me not to leave, he hadn't meant it, he wanted me to stay. I just said that is not an option. Move her in if you want. I'm off. Chip was astounded and at first didn't think I meant it. But I did, I moved, and it didn't take long for Carly to start spending time at his. How did I know? Because I rented a room at Chip's mother's house. So, he could not bring Carly there because that is where I was, and his mother did not like her anyway.

Chip told me that he was taking her to Italy, not me. I spoke to Gary who was booked to go, and asked if he would be willing to take me as a pillion, my Z400 not being big enough for the trip. I had my pillion ticket and she was not taking my holiday from me. I told Chip that I was still going and he was obviously worried as having a couple of warrior women was not his idea of fun. *He needn't have worried because she was not going to be going anyway.* He said he has already asked her and she wanted to go. I shrugged and said I was not arguing about it. I had a plan. I retrieved my self-esteem a couple of weeks later. I went back to the coast one evening and after going out with a few friends I shinned up a few seaside street lamps and acquired some lovely coloured light bulbs from the seafront. I carefully wrapped them up and took them home. The next night I waited until Carly and Chip went out for the night, I still had my key to the house, so let myself in. I changed each and every light bulb in the house for a nice coloured one, red in the bedroom, green in the living room, blue in the kitchen, orange in the hallway and yellow in the bathroom. The white bulbs were put on the back step and crushed. Apparently she was not happy that I still had a key to the house and knowing Chip was not averse to eating his cake and still keeping it, she assumed he was still seeing me. She hadn't even lasted a month. This was the only time I ever went back to someone after leaving them. Carly vacated the house. Chip was a bit peeved but did admit it was quite funny, the one thing he had missed was my sense of humour.

With the status quo restored, I moved back to Chip's house and a truce was declared between us. We agreed, if either of us found someone else and wanted to move on, we should be honest and just say so. My life was repaired, with a get out clause in the background for both of us. The main thing established was no sharing. I was pleased that my efforts culminated with me having my holiday and keeping the roof over my head. Things were not easy, as once hurt I find it difficult to trust anyone who I feel has betrayed me, but we found a way forward which suited us both. The much anticipated holiday was only a couple of weeks away, and boy did I need it now.

Chapter 8 Travelling (Not So Plain Sailing After All)

Being a naturally happy person, I did not stay in the dumps for long, and who could be, when I had my holiday to Italy. The group all arrived at Chip's in the morning, ready to ride to Harwich together. All the luggage was repacked between the four bikes. There were six of us going, and it was difficult to tell which of us was the more excited. Hans and I were both riding pillion as our own bikes were smaller and not really big enough to keep up. Chip, Gary, Sonny and Jonathan were riding their bikes, respectively the Kawasaki Z1, Triumph T150, Triumph T160 and a 750 Commando Fastback. So, all packed, ready, steady, go, go, go......

We set off and had a comfortable ride down to the ferry in Harwich. With plenty of time we were relaxed and happy, the sun shone for a change and the horizon there to spur us forward. We had all been to the Isle of Man previously so putting our machinery onto the ferry was not new to us, we were given side slots where our bikes could be tied down safely. As we were boarded first we got our tickets checked and were shown to our shared overnight cabin. Having seen the queue for car and lorry boarders we dumped our hand luggage and made haste to get to the canteen areas so we could have a bite to eat and then get our heads down ready for an early start. We got the maps out, and wrote a quick list of towns to head for, made sure we had some tape to put the lists on top of the tank bags so that we knew what roads to take and tried to sleep. It was not easy as the excitement of actually being on the start of our journey did not encourage common sense, eventually we did manage some rest.

I always sleep deeply so left the lads to wake me up when the boat came in sight of land. We went upstairs to get a good breakfast to speed up the first leg of riding. Good job we did. The worst of being first onboard made us have to wait while the other vehicles disembarked first in order to give us room to untie and manoeuvre the bikes around so we could ride off. With full tanks of fuel – all giving the heads up – we set off. It was surprisingly easy to find our way as the main routes were well signed and we were going to use the 'autobahns' for ease, although we hoped to take in some lesser roads as we thought motorways might be boring for the whole trip. We had a lot to learn. Our first stop was found to be about 140 miles down the road and we were only just out of Holland. The services seemed pleasant and we all fuelled up, going into the shop to get drinks and something to eat. I had a milkshake, but the boys all ordered coffee. Their faces when they were served with a black substance in a dolls size cup and saucer. The cost was about three times what we would pay for a coffee in dear old England. After a heated exchange with the waiters, we were told that a mug size coffee was called coffee 'mit milch' or café con leche. Lesson learned and we decided that we should grab a snack and make headway.

The day became quite a journey, very different from the idyllic tour we had imagined as we had a day and a half to get to our chalets in Sorrento. The distances slowly dawning on us as we hit each of the towns on our lists, and there being multiple numbers on the sign posts to our next destination. 150, next 125, next 95, next 130 and on it went. It dawned on us that a couple of inches on a map computed to so much more. As the day wore on we were realising that we had bitten off much more than we could chew. Our own mission impossible. The numbers on the sign posts flashed past and we seemed to be making good progress until we realised that they represented kilometers which were shorter than miles, but it did help make it seem we were getting along well. About halfway through the day it dawned on us that it was a lot further than our initial perception. Oh no, the trips on our speedos were telling us we done about 450 miles and we were still not quite halfway down Germany. It was going to be a long day and we had to get more or less to Italy for our night stop. Sorrento had a cutoff point of 2pm the following day in order to collect our keys to paradise. Our pleasant meandering tour through Europe was a madcap ride on the autobahns, pushing an average of 125 miles between a crazed rushed fuel, drink, snack stop. No time to look about, get on and ride, no time to rest. Our backsides were aching, but we had to ride.

Luckily the weather was pleasant but other than that we were stressed. I was relieved that it was their idea – even though I had been instrumental in organizing the logistics. The order of each stop became monotonous, stop, fuel up, hit the expensive drink and snack machines which were quicker than queueing for a proper sit down meal. Then the cry of the day was ready, go, no time for steady as anxiety and tiredness started to be felt by all. We aimed and passed towns we had heard of, Frankfurt, Stuttgart, hitting Bern and Switzerland in the dark. Riding into Switzerland about dusk we needed to fill up in a town without visible life. We eventually found a garage lit up, great – maybe not – no server, pumps were on but did not work, would not take money – they only accepted certain card membership. Really tired by this time we were stumped, until a Swiss gentleman in a swanky porsche came to our rescue, he kindly filled all our bikes, worked out how much it all cost and we all gave him our cash – probably paying over the odds with conversion calculations. Never mind, we had fuel and only had the rest of the Alps to navigate. By now it was about 9.30pm, we were tired but we pressed on. As we rode we had spectacular glimpses of Lake Lucerne and the lights of the towns as these reflected prettily in the waters on the far side of the lake. Soon enough we were riding through the Gotthard tunnel. Not being able to find a B&B in the area we had no choice, we carried on through the night.

It was spectacular as dawn approached. Heading down the tricky, twisty mountain roads towards Italy we were all on the point of exhaustion and to carry on was getting quite dangerous. Jonathan nearly came off as he almost went to sleep. We came to a small village close to the border and we hit dirt, literally. We found a small mound of relatively smooth grass, parked up and out came our 'bin bags'. The boys giggled but they were big enough to fit three each in one bag. Fully clothed we dived in with our feet out of the open end. I think we were all asleep within about five seconds of lying down. We were out for the count and slept soundly for just under four hours – as each of us woke due to extreme discomfort – we were all drenched. Our clothes were wet as we crawled out of our bags. We couldn't understand what had happened as it had not rained – the roads were dry – all around us was dry. It was still early morning, but the sun coming up had covered us as we snuggled in our BLACK bin bags. With our breathing the condensation had soaked us – clothes and jackets – socks – everything. We couldn't believe it. We sat in the sun for about half an hour hoping to dry out a bit, but then we decided to move on and dry out while covering the miles. After about another hour of travelling down the mountainsides we found a garage, fuelled up, fed and watered, a lot cheaper in Italy than Germany and Switzerland, and sped onwards once again.

Now that it was daylight we could rejoice in the beautiful scenery and roads and although not having had much sleep we were in better fettle. We got happier as we dried out and found some good cafes near the roadside garages which lightened our moods. Some of the viaducts, aqueducts and bridges, churches, and general views were the best tonic and reminded us why we were here. The only problem was the telephone numbers on the road signs – but we made progress, passing Florence, Milan and then Rome – this gave us the impetus to allow a quick detour as we were all quite intent on seeing the Colosseum – having seen all the films this was a must see and we were the closest we would ever be to it. Knowing what we did now about the distances on maps, we knew we only had this one chance, a day trip from Sorrento was not going to be possible. Detouring off the main motorway somehow we managed to get to the center of Rome, embarrassed ourselves with the locals by stopping to ask where the Colosseum was for a lady to point over our shoulders to the monument. As if it wasn't big enough to see as the spectacular building towered above us, we managed to park up and all bought tickets to have a look around this icon. We were lucky enough to be allowed to clamber around the terraces and walk on the boards above the animal pits which had not long been discovered back then. Our legs were stretched to our hearts content as we had a whistlestop tour of the ruins, but then we hurried back to our bikes to get going.

The last leg towards Naples and the Amalfi coast was spectacular but again we were trying to hit an almost impossible deadline. So, back to our 120mile routine, with lovely fresh snacks at each stop we tiredly reached our goal – just.

The chalet manager was not happy with us as we made her late for her siesta, but grudgingly she gave us the keys, showed us the allotted huts and disappeared. We just fell in the doors and crashed, not to be seen until the next day.

In the morning Gary looked at his trip meter, we had done over 1500 miles in 36 hours. In comparison it had taken Stu and I ten days to do a similar mileage on the Isle of Man. We all looked at each other, astounded. That was incredible on the bikes we were riding, poor Jon looked at his Commando with pride that it had made it that far as it was the oldest bike between us.

We decided no more riding for the day, walking and looking about was what we wanted. First things first, we wanted food so we went off to find a bakery, then get some fruit and vegetables. This accomplished, we headed back to the chalets and had our first real feel of being on holiday. The relief that we didn't have to ride any further that day. Our Z1 had finally had enough of non-stop riding and had started 'pinking' during the last couple of hundred miles so Chip did a bit of tinkering only to find the bike spluttered and died. The lads all put their heads together and worked out the coil on one side had quit. It had succumbed to the heat of 36 hours almost continual running and the heat of the Italian sunshine finished it off. The next few hours were wasted trying to get in contact with ACI, the Italian version of the RAC who were responsible under our international breakdown insurance. They tried to be helpful but it was difficult because we were in Italy and it wasn't a Moto Guzzi or Ducati. They could order in the part but it would take three weeks to get to us. Err, we had to get to the Adriatic in one week's time. Sorry, but that is all we can do was the unhelpful reply.

We resorted to panic as the immediate answer to emergency fall out. But bikers are always resilient and eventually we decided to see if we could find a garage and devise some sort of resolution. There were no big garages in the vicinity but there was a little one man band with a workshop about half a mile away. Great. Only option available so it had to be delved into. Little chap found, does not speak English. I stepped up with my Spanish and happily the dialogues of our respective Spanish/Italian rescued the day. We had brought the offending coil with us, the description of caput sufficed, I tried to explain the Kawasaki Z1 as the offending vehicle and the chap took the coil from us, saying come back tomorrow morning. He had a lovely smile, but we were a tad worried and not too confident, but again, nothing else presented hope. However, much to our delight our chap came good, and in that few hours he worked a miracle and somehow rebuilt the coil. I guess engineers in rural areas make do and mend all the time. He would not accept payment and just told us to go try it, which we did, and much to our relief it worked – not even flickering in hesitation. We took a few bottles of wine back on the bike and he took a good look around the Kawasaki as he had not seen one before.

The following day was time to do a bit of sightseeing so back on the bikes. We had a lovely ride around the Amalfi coast and while stopped for a bit of lunch at a roadside café were amazed at how many mopeds were flying around, with whole families aboard – small children between mum and dad, a couple standing over the frame in front of the rider and holding the dash with another one or two ensconced on the carrier. It was quite something to see, some of the teenagers were riding hell for leather around the tight corners with their girlfriends riding side saddle behind them, barely holding on. Unbelievable but fascinating how carefree they all rode.

We finished our welcome break and continued around the coast until we eventually saw some signs for Pompei – Gary and I had both heard about this town and we dutifully paid it a visit. The people who had been petrified at the moment of their deaths was quite breathtaking and awe inspiring. You could see the faces almost screaming in terror as they fell victims to the volcano erupting in the distance. We had a few hours looking around, walking the streets, seeing into the houses and looking at some of the elaborate tiled floors and walls. It really made you think that life is precious and to be lived. As we got back to the car park we all looked up to the mountain in the distance. It gave us the initiative to have a visit to Vesuvius, so that was the plan for the next trip out. We bought a local map and decided that we would have to go through Naples, which seemed a good place to see as well.

Having ridden around the coast we decided to look for somewhere to go swimming, and once we were nearly back to our chalets we stopped and asked a couple of lads who were walking down the road with towels slung over their shoulders. They told us where to go for a good swim, we followed their directions and found a lovely old port area with several people swimming around in the water. No discussion needed, we all jumped into the water to cool off. This was the opportunity for the first discord between us. From hot to cooler water – we all have our differences of how to get wet. I love the water and am a good swimmer, but I hate to be splashed with cold water before I am ready. Hans in a burst of fun decided to splash me and in true form I retaliated, strongly; annoyed, I grabbed him and shoved him off his feet into the water, I proceeded to hold him down whereupon he panicked and fought for his life. He could not swim and was terrified I was going to drown him. When he managed to regain his feet I realised he had been quite frightened – realising his real terror I apologised and we agreed to try not to upset the other again. He accepted that his action of splashing me was not the best thing he had done, I accepted my reaction was a bit extreme too, but it was instinctive in me to retaliate when I felt threatened. Hans had remembered by this time one of my nick names was Thumper so he should have known better.

Our trip to the volcano the next day was again a great experience. The road up to the highest car park was quite eventful as most of it was a very loose gravel road, with hairpins and not much width, definitely meant for cars – not bikes. It was a treacherous road and we were all relieved when we reached the top. Our intrepid group got into adventure mode as we all declined the cable lift, we became sherpas and scrambled up to the crater. It was quite unnerving to see the steam coming out of this hole, and realising that it was not extinct but dormant. Suddenly it put Pompei into perspective for us. We thought that it would be good to find somewhere to have a meal and that once we descended back down the mountain it would be nice to go into Naples.

Having got used to the erratic 'racing' style of Italian driving, we were still astonished with the amount of traffic and total chaos in Naples, there did not seem to be any system nor any rules in place, once in the central square area it was every vehicle for themselves. There were trams which had their timetables – they went at their speed and everyone else beware. The general melee meant that every vehicle seemed to compete for any spare bit of road and just dived into it without a care for other road users. As for driving on the left or right, if they knew which was which they did not seem to adhere to any of it. I don't think there was a rule book, if there was then no-one had read it. We got into a jam as the rear wheel caught in a tram track and would not release us, with a tram bearing down on us we thought we were going to get run over, but at the last minute and a lot of throttle we got away with inches to spare. Italian driving is frightening at the best of times, but that incident is still heartbeat stopping just remembering the moment. I really thought we'd had it. By the time we got to the plaza we were more than ready to find a restaurant and gather our wits again.

With our better knowledge of distances we tried to prepare ourselves for the middle road trip across to Rimini and our second part of the journey. This time, we knew better, we asked how far it was. Oh, we were told, two days, about 500 miles. Undaunted, knowing we had covered three times that in 36 hours, it should perhaps take 12 hours. If we set off early we could ride six hours have a leisurely lunch, and take the second half of the ride in two sections getting to Rimini by about seven or eight o'clock. Yep, we concurred. Another long day in the saddle, but then a whole week to leisurely enjoy the beaches, we only wanted one day to visit San Marino and see where the grand prix track was as there was no racing imminent.

We set off with optimism, but it wasn't long before the roads diminished in both size and widths, with ever decreasing quality of road surface while the roadside cliffs got steeper and steeper. The 500 plus miles were definitely not main road territory, but up and over the central mountain range. The roads were often not much more than small tracks with narrow hairpins a plenty. We did it in our intrepid gung ho way and got to Rimini – without a leisurely mid ride break. Had it been possible we would have stopped somewhere for lunch, but the roads were so remote and rural we couldn't find any cafés. We arrived at our destination about midnight and had to find our landlord who had given up on us and gone to a party. It was early morning before we could enter our apartment and crash once again. Who would have thought we would be caught out once more after out epic 36hour stint. Never mind, we're the Brits, we can do anything.

Rimini was very much a lazy beach town, with loads of lovely Italian ice cream. The flavours were varied so I consequently found a need to try each and every one. Ooh, the chocolate chip, the toffee, banana, rum and raisin, coffee, chocolate, strawberry, tutti-frutti, nuts and just about every flavour imaginable. I could not get enough and developed a speed in my endeavours as I had to eat them before they melted in the heat. I coped, quite well I thought, as I batch tested from all the many ice cream vendors dotted around the town. Chip was getting more and more agitated as he thought about the expense. Never mind, as far as I was concerned it was my money, my comfort and who was he to tell me what to do. Eventually his temper fanned during the heated evenings and as I approached the umpteenth stall he grabbed my purse before I had a chance to order my next treat. I was furious, absolutely incensed, and by the time we got back to our flat war broke out between us. I packed my bags, prepared to leave and stay in Italy (Agostini lived there, so I thought I would too). As I was packing Chip found my passport and refused to give it back, he still had my purse too. Well, that was it, I launched myself at him and my language was definitely not nice, Chip was calling for help but the lads shut us in our bedroom and left him to it. They were not going to get involved. I eventually retrieved my things, and stalked out of the premises totally intending to stay in Europe even if it was midnight. A couple of the lads came after me, not wanting to abandon me in these foreign lands. In deference to them and their feelings of chivalry I calmed down and broodily went back to the flat with them, knowing that it was not fair to let them worry about me. I kept my purse close to me after that and made it clear that what I did with my money was my business and that Chip was not to interfere with my spending decisions. My defence was that I enjoyed every ice cream to the full, and I was not loading the bike up with unnecessary clothing or handbag products etc.

We did have a much more relaxed week on the Adriatic and as we looked at the map towards the end of it, as far as we could see, we were about 500 miles closer to Ostend for the return journey, and we knew that most of those roads were the quick autobahns so the drill was calculated and we were convinced it would not take much more time than our trip from Amalfi to Rimini due to the better roads. We would know what we were in for this time – about seven or eight 125 mile ride/stop stints – so no real worries confronting us. Although we would like to see Venice on the way back this was acknowledged to perhaps be a stretch too far for our itinerary. We would take our cue on the road home. How could we have been so optimistic?

Duly rested and ready for an early start home, we set our alarms and the bikes were packed as I went round the corner to the bakery for some breakfast to set us up for the road. Last cups of coffee and milkshake for me, we set off in good mood. This time we were going to go through Austria via the Brenner Pass. Although we did ride up the Adriatic coast towards Venice we accepted that we did not have the time to visit this iconic town and veered off on the main road to Verona, then Innsbruck, Brenner and Munich heading north. Plan all set, looking forward to a long day riding. Ready, steady – oh no. As we hit the Italian Austrian border area the skies opened and we took refuge near a roadside shop in order to don any waterproofs we had. A couple of the boys had lightweight waterproof overalls but I did not. I looked around for something suitable but there was nothing immediately obvious. However, emergency the mother of inventions, black bin bags. They held the moisture in when we tried to sleep, perhaps they would hold the water out – optimistically I bought a pack of them, and I also bought a couple of bungees. Poking two holes in the bottom, I put my legs in one bag and held it with a bungee, with three holes in the second bag it was head in middle, arms in each side and bungee around middle over the bottom bag. Yeah, 'job's a good'un. The lads all fell about laughing at me, but I was happy that mostly I would keep dryish.

After a couple of ride/fuel sprints in torrential rain it didn't look any brighter as we looked northwards. We hoped that by the time we went through the Brenner Pass we would be on the other side of the mountains and that would be it, but no. The Brenner Pass was great as there was obviously no rain inside, but when we eventually came out on the other side, the heavens were still aiming at us. It turned out that we were to be rained upon nearly all the way to the Netherlands. The worst casualty bike wise was poor Jonathan's Commando which was not happy, he was putting nearly as much oil in it as petrol on that wet ride home. We endured well over 600 miles of torrential rain. A fitting end to our holiday, drowned rats eagerly waiting on the dockside to get onboard the ship. Jonathan relieved his Commando had been coaxed to the ferry. The last laugh was when we took our waterproofs off. The one piece overalls the boys wore were not very good – all had leaked at seams and zip points – whereas my bin bags had kept my torso snug and dry – I may have looked ridiculous but at least I was not chattering with wet cold clothing around my middle, my arms were the worst, but I had ridden with my arms over my legs, gloves over my knees so they were not as bad. A few hours on board the boat, a good meal in the restaurant with bits and bobs on the radiators near us, and we were comfortable enough to enjoy a few hours of sleep before getting back to England. What a fortnight, what a ride, and what an experience. Never again will I trust a map to work out distances, inches do not show miles. I bought a pencil size wheel to calculate for any future excursions we may go for, although I was definitely drawn towards a flying holiday next.

Chapter 9 The Calm After The Storm

C hip and I had sorted out a lot of our problems, but I had a lot of soul-searching to do. Obviously there was some discord between us in respect of what we wanted from life, and I was never going to be the obedient woman in his life. I had my insecurities as my trust had been damaged and although I had stability with both work and a home, none of it was really that secure long term. There was no hurry to do anything and I kept putting money away for the time when things went wrong, as by now I had learned that I couldn't really rely on anyone else, only me, and for that a bit of financial security was a priority.

We still enjoyed our evenings out with our mates, we had a lot of anecdotal mileage with our tales of Italy and travel inspired many a story of our exploits. We had all enjoyed how easy it was to cross the channel and just drive wherever we wished to go. The big lesson learned was obviously plenty of time was needed as the distances were vast, the need for night stops was emphasized as the danger of accidents when pushing ourselves to the limit was real. We had got away with it this trip, but only by the skin of our teeth. For the following year we continued our ride outs with the guys, fun nights bowling were a regular pastime, and there were the occasional dance nights and we entered into a variety of pastimes. As ever, there was always something to attract us and fill our weekends.

One of the wives in the group was a great woman and I spent a lot of time with her, especially as her husband was one of Chip's personal friends. They were both bikers, and when I passed my bike test Hanna was the first friend game enough to go on the back of me. We decided to go shopping and she gaily got on the pillion to travel into the city. All went well until riding up Grape's Hill in Norwich I suddenly realised I had forgotten my glasses. We got to the market place and while wandering around I confessed my sin, Hanna laughed until she suddenly realised what that meant. She asked me, 'can you see alright to ride then?' I replied, 'of course I can see, just not that good as I'm short sighted'. She looked at me, 'how can you tell what traffic is around you?' My reply was as honest as I could be. 'The big blobs are buses, middle size ones are cars, and I can hear the motorbikes!' She was not impressed by that, but I had got it into her head that if I could ride, then so could she. It wasn't long before she got a small bike, passed her bike test and got herself a Honda 400/4. I was so proud of her, and she never looked back (unless I was behind her).

As time wore on I started taking note of how Chip and I differed. Although we had a lot in common, music was not one of them. I preferred the raucous dance with Rock and Roll 1950s style, my favourite. Chip was not that much of a fan, even though he was seven years older than myself and it should have been his era. His preference was to my mind a bit dreary and sad (depressing), Leonard Cohen and Bob Dylan were his records of choice, backed up by Gene Pitney who I learned to really love, and also Roy Orbison who again was really appreciated by me. There was not much other music which we both liked to listen to but I was always quite happy to have my head in a book so it was not insurmountable. With us in a routine of being out and about most of the weekends it did not really make much difference. We got into a bit of a lazy working week in, weekends out, no real burdens or responsibilities and we got along companionably for the next year.

I absolutely enjoyed my Kawasaki, commuting five days a week, sometimes going to see my mates midweek if football was on the telly. I was regularly riding a couple of hundred miles every week, all year round. I had a top box for bits and bobs, and enjoyed going out whenever I felt like it. I had a few round trips of about forty miles which I rode just for the joy of it. Riding to the top of a hill, to then ride to the next hill which in Norfolk that could qualify as a trek. This was my freedom and the feeling of being in control has never wavered for me. On one of my shopping trips I was thinking about where I would like to go next, so I went to the travel agents and got a few brochures to see what was on offer. I wanted to travel further afield so riding thousands of miles was not the relaxing trip I felt we needed to do. My bike was not fast enough to keep up with the lads and I knew it was not viable for Chip to think of me riding off into the sunset on my own. It had been traumatic for him last year when I had taken myself off to Brighton while he was procrastinating. A package tour was what we needed, so brochures on the coffee table it was.

Chip was a real sun-seeker and the heat of southern Europe had appealed to his inner sun-god. We spent a couple of weeks before choosing Greece, we booked a two week trip to Athens for the early summer. We were flying from Luton, and to save money Chip had an old workmate who worked at the fire station at the airport who would get authority for us to park at his staff car park. Again, to save money, we went on the bike. Luggage restrictions were easily kept to as we couldn't carry that much on the Z1, the bonus of this was his mates were there 24/7 keeping his precious steed safe while we were away. Packing was not a problem as we only needed T-shirts, shorts, swimwear. Chip was a bit unsure as he had not flown before, but we both looked forward to it. On arrival at the Luton Fire Depot we were met by Chip's mate who not only settled our bike safe inside the depot, introduced us to his workmates and had arranged an airside lift to the terminal and collection back to the fire depot when we got back. No worries while we were away, we had a personal guard for the bike – for free. Who could ask for more?

We got off to a good start, joined the queues at the airport and looked forward to this holiday. The flight was interesting as Chip had never flown before. He started to worry when looking out the window, we were just behind the wings and he was alarmed when the plane sped up on the runway before taking off. We had a window seat and he couldn't believe the bouncing of the metal of the wings as they flexed visibly against the strength of the wind on them. He initially panicked when he saw the flaps move, not knowing that this was normal to get lift off. I had flown before and was amused, but Chip soon got into the stride of it and relaxed once the plane was airborne. Thankfully the flight was uneventful, and he marveled as we travelled over land and sea, looking over the coasts as we crossed the channel trying to assimilate what he was seeing with maps studied before we left home. By the time we got towards the end of the flight we were both more than ready to get off the plane and stretch our legs. The heat hit us and made us draw breath, we had not appreciated such a quick change of temperature. Luckily we were not going to be far from Athens, and it was just a short coach trip to our hotel, and the swimming pool which enticed us as soon as we could unpack and jump in.

We had a great holiday, and took a few trips to some of the ruins along the coast, including the Acropolis during the daytime, and a 'sun and light' performance of the Greek history of Athens where we were given a talk about various battles with some of the surrounding monuments and ruins being lit up – this was quite spectacular in the dark and brought the buildings to life. The beach was as expected and our hotel had a pool which we enjoyed several times during the day. The hotel had traditional dancing at night and generally was a normal mediterranean break. The one thing which Chip and I were amazed at was while we swam in the rooftop pool, the aircraft were flying so low on landing and take-off we were able to see the passengers in the windows of the planes, we could actually wave to them and they to us. Being bikers, the noise of these planes never disturbed us, but fascinated us that the planes were actually able to fly at all. On one of our shopping trips to the market in Athens I bought a couple of bronze statues without giving a thought to getting them home on the bike, but in the end I just bought a shoulder bag to carry them home. Chip just raised his eyebrows at me and chose not to comment, just mumbled about weight and the bike was not a donkey kind of stuff.

After our amazing trip to Greece, routine and reality set in again, life was getting back to normal. Although I had grave concerns about what the future would hold; I still had the spectre from last year of Carly, and how easy it had been for Chip to wander; as far as I was concerned that episode made me unsure of what to do. I decided to enjoy the life we had, but I had to save towards getting myself in a position of safety. To my mind that always comes with a price tag. I had to get myself into a workable situation for true independence. I was partly there with my motorbike, but I needed more than that going forward. I worked hard in the factory and put some of my monies aside – my next goal was to pass my driving test – my theory was that it will never get easier, nor will it get cheaper – so before I was burdened with more responsibility I needed driving lessons.

Chapter 10 The Road Ahead, Choppy Waters

Fate had other plans and delayed my car driving aspirations. I had an accident on my Z400. The day started normally, but after a brilliantly hot summer the weather broke and the rains started. I was on my way to work and approached a roundabout. As I tried to slow down the brakes appeared to not be working. The road was slippery as the oils had come to the surface and the wet had turned them into an almost ice like consistency. Not only that, but I was not used to disc brakes. The discs were covered in a wet surface and therefore did not grab the wheel as expected, there was an action delay. So, it felt like the bike was not stopping, I squeezed the brakes harder just as they broke through the wet film, and hey presto – crash bang wallop – I was downed as the pads gripped the discs simultaneously.

My dignity suffered as I found I couldn't pick the bike up. It hurt too much. Even worse, a condescending man came who did come to my help dug in with a distained retort about 'a woman should not ride a bike if she couldn't pick it up herself'. The reason I couldn't wasn't because the bike was too heavy, but a kindly nurse who also came to my aid checked me over. I had broken my collar bone badly. No wonder I was hurting. I had to leave the bike there while I was taken to casualty. At the hospital I was able to let Chip know I'd had the accident, so he arranged for someone to collect my bike which luckily had fared better than I had. It was slightly scuffed but not too broken. I had my shoulder strapped up and my arm put in a sling for about four weeks. Chip explained the way the brakes had worked differently to how my Bantam did so I realised it was just my naivety that caused the accident, not totally my fault, just different operating procedures needed understanding.

While I was unable to work for the duration of my shoulder injury I spent much of my time with one of my best friends at that time. Tina was with a new chap in her life, and he not only worked, but lived in the car world. Under his influence she had car lessons and managed to pass her driving test. Tina is one of those people with a chirpy, cheerful outlook on life. She failed her first test, but was not keen to tell me why initially. It turned out that she had a few minor errors, but in her anxiety she had gone to grab the gearshift and by mistake got hold of the examiner's knee. Believing that this had been a ploy he marked her down and failed her. The second test she knew not to make that mistake again and somehow she got through. We had a great laugh about this and I was hopeful I could save myself this problem. She gave me the details of her driving instructor so I followed that up, and booked my first lesson – I was going to start with two hours, once a week, on a Saturday afternoon. I figured that Chip would be distracted and not be too bothered by my absence while he watched his beloved football.

The Saturday came around and I had made sure that Chip would have his snacks by his armchair, settled him down for his ritualistic box watching. I had booked my lesson for two o'clock so that I would be back around the end of the match, ready to go to see Dave's parents before our night ride out. Instead of staying in his chair, when I said I was going out for a couple of hours he decided to see me off. Ouch. I had not actually admitted where I was going due to the nuisance he made when I wanted a larger motorbike, and thought he would assume I was going shopping as I often did. When he saw a driving instructor turn up to collect me he went mad. He thought that was a waste of money as he had a car and drove when we needed to go anywhere. We had a small dispute there and then, but as time was money I jumped in the passenger seat and told the instructor to drive – quickly.

My instructor drove about half a mile down the road and then we swapped seats and my lessons began. I was enjoying myself and looking forward to taking my test. I was very confident as I had had a few hours with mother a couple of years beforehand, but also I was over confident as I had been riding my bikes for nearly three years now. Speed was my favorite part of being on the road, and I had a few lessons scaring my instructor to bits. Although for the first couple of lessons we kept to quiet rural roads until he was confident I could manage the foot pedals, steering and gear changes, I needed to learn the finer points of roadcraft; I especially needed to drive more carefully on busy roads, due diligence with other traffic etc. I was happily careering about on the town roads with cars parked both sides, driving far quicker than my ability to react, but to start with my instructor dare not take control in case I panicked and swerved into the cars alongside our trajectory. At the end of the road he directed me to park up and gave me a telling off. I did try to explain that I was used to going at that speed on my motorbike. He reminded me that a car was wider and I could hurt someone, especially if they opened their doors to get out of the parked cars. Point taken.

Having been duly reprimanded I did my best to be a model pupil as I realised it would take me longer to get my licence if I did not listen, (listening to others has never been my strong point). I was really excited about getting this essential tool of life and no-one (ie Chip) was going to stop me doing what a girl needs to do. It did cause a bit of friction in the homestead and for the first few lessons I just did not tell Chip when I was going driving. The following Saturday I said I was going shopping on the bus, consequently he walked me to the bus stop to make sure I got on the bus. However, half expecting trouble I took the precaution of arranging to meet the instructor at the shops next stop down the road. Chip said he would pick me up in town to save the bus fare home, I agreed to meet him at the entrance to the Co-op in town at 5.30pm. I went off on my lesson, and the instructor agreed to drop me off in town as needed. All went well, we swapped seats so I was back in the passenger seat as we approached the Co-op, I saw Chip, he was looking at his watch and luckily didn't see me. I was dropped at the lower door, quickly got out and before he could moan at me I walked uphill to where he was and told him off for waiting at the wrong door. Phew. That was another fine mess I managed to get out of.

It did annoy me that I had to use a bit of subterfuge to do what I wanted and after a couple of sessions I bit the bullet and told Chip that I was continuing my driving lessons. At first he was adamant that it was a waste of money, but I pointed out that it was my life, and after the Carly debacle I couldn't rely on him to always being there for me. He thought that episode was done and dusted, so it made him a bit wary, but as I pointed out I had to make sure I could look after myself as I couldn't really rely on anyone else. Being quite pragmatic he accepted that, although he swore blind he would not mess me around again. I acknowledged his intent, but he would have to accept that I had a right to look after myself, and reminded him that he was the one who made me come back from Italy when I wanted to stay there. If he wanted me to stay, then I had to be allowed to follow my own path too. A truce was called and I continued my lessons.

Although I was not in a position to buy my own car at least I would be in a position of just finding one when I had the money now. Chip was not prepared to let me drive his car if I got my licence so having my own vehicle would have to wait. This stubbornness on his part did not bode well, and although I didn't have the money to buy a car, that would have to wait. Also, I could imagine the opposition I would get while looking to get my own car, getting my 'bigger' bike had been difficult enough and I really did not want to upset the status quo in our household at that time. Well, not until I was ready. I had already learned that everyone else seemed to look after themselves first. My horns would have to stay sheathed until money caught up with my wishes.

Chapter 11 Where Do I Go From Here?

Once I had secured my driving licence it was time to look at my plans for the future. Analyzing the options at my disposal I decided that I definitely did want a family in the future and Chip was absolutely not interested in being a father. This was something that was not negotiable for either of us, I felt that it was time to make a decision. By this time we had been together for about two years and although we had a good life it was time for me to move on. The differences in our ways was becoming more obvious and I also knew I wanted more fun and laughter. I really missed the dances which Chip did not like. He wasn't really comfortable with my independent streak, in fact it alarmed him that I wanted to do so much. The football was really not my bag, and it was grating on me that I had to use my 'unnecessary' bike to take the washing to the launderette in order to avoid having to watch a match, but the biggest difference was the family one. I looked around to try and find somewhere else to live and got myself a small bedsit. I packed myself up and moved my belongings before discussing things with Chip. Although a sad time, it was over, we remained good friends through the years, never falling out.

A couple of weeks after leaving Chip I was lucky enough to pass my car test. Although I was not in a position to have my own car at least I was in a position of just finding one when I had the money, the hardest bit was achieved and money was the only obstacle. Now with my own key to my life, I was totally free to do what I wanted. I had started spending more time with my friends, especially Tina. The world of cars beckoned and this was her world. Her husband John was a stock car driver and the weekends now included car racing. Naturally after passing my test the first person I wanted to tell was my best friend. She was so pleased for me and we were busy chatting when her fella came home with a mate. The mate had a messengering job to do which meant he had to collect some documents about 6pm, then drive up to Chesterfield to get them signed first thing in the morning, and return them to Norwich by 10am the next day. He was a bit anxious as he had not slept but needed to drive all night to get there, probably not get much sleep before getting the paperwork signed at six in the morning with a long drive back. He had a mate who would normally go and share the driving with him but he wasn't able to go. Not a problem I said, I'll come if you like. He asked if I had a full licence and I gaily said Yes, omitting that I had only just passed my test two hours prior.

John looked at Tina who nodded her head so he didn't raise any objections. Paul was happy to have another driver on the trip so he went to collect the documents needed, while I looked at the map that John kept at home. I noted the towns to be driven through and listed them in order, went home to change my clothes and was back at Tina's ready for my first bone fide road trip. Excited at the prospect of my first driving experience without the obligatory L plates. Paul returned and yet another adventure started. He was relieved that I had researched the route and the weather was good. The horizon awaited the intrepid crew as we set off. Paul drove all the way there while I navigated and we made relatively good time, stopping on the way for snacks and then a good meal just before we hit Chesterfield. We found the address and as it was now late and dark we got ready to put the seats in recliner mode and had a couple of blankets for cover while we both had a sleep, Paul had an alarm clock to make sure we were ready in good time for the morning. We got the documents signed and I was to take the first drive so that Paul could be fully rested as I had been able to doze on the journey the day before.

I was so elated to be able to drive without having supervision and due to my motorcycling was quite capable of navigating the return trip by myself. We came back across country and down the A1, A17 and A47 and I was feeling pleased with myself. The only little mishap was on one of the non-dual carriageway roads where a holdup made the traffic very slow. We were in a mini, and I had a huge Mercedes lorry tailgating me. Being quite annoyed with this, as I knew he was deliberately trying to unnerve me, I slowed down to give myself a better braking distance, which the lorry driver took exception to. All I could see in my mirror was the bottom half of the Mercedes badge he was so close. Paul happened to wake up at this time and he turned his head to look over his shoulder and was alarmed to see how close the lorry behind us was. He tried to urge me to drive quicker, which was futile as the traffic was still driving slowly and I was not going to give up my braking space just because he was nervous. After that we pulled in for fuel and a snack and Paul took back his precious little car. Once our trip was finished successfully he drove me back to get my bike at Tina's. His face was a picture when John told him I'd only passed my test the day before.

This interval period in my life opened up a new vision of fame and glory. I was interested in all things in the petrol head world. I had a few mates who were involved in Speedway and a connection of the garage where I worked, I had the opportunity to try out as a Speedway Rider, for the King's Lynn team. It was offered to me as a 'token' chance, but I surprised the then boss of the team to offer me a 'ride'. It was tempting but I had not been that impressed with the fact that there were no brakes on these quick machines. That probably contributed to me having fairly good trial times. Also, I had seen gravel rash on friends by this time and the thought of sliding off on the shale track was not that attractive, so I left that idea on the bench.

The next chance to enter the racing world with in the Banger Race world. I was offered the loan of a friend's car for the 'ladies race'. This was to be a four lap race, at a track just outside of Norwich. The first race I won by two laps, and was awarded a hairdryer for a prize. The second race I won by a good margin but only got a box of chocolates as first prize. I like chocolates, but the prizes were going downhill. Anyhow, the other women were not enamoured with me for knocking them out of the way as I was fairly aggressive in my attitude to the racing and they refused to let me race after that. I guess my friend was not too happy with his 'banger' car being bashed about on my way to fame. Again, another avenue not for me.

My introduction to driving four wheels was quick. By the end of the first week I had popped home to tell my mother and stepfather I had passed my test, and mum asked if I would drive her and a friend to London as they were booked to see a show. This was an offer not to be refused as I would have the car to myself for three days before collecting them for the trip home. Another friend was to look after stepfather and my brother for the weekend. Mother thought she was doing me a favour and would show me how to drive in the capital but she soon realised I was confident enough to compete with the black cab drivers on the busy roads. Life held no fears for me, even if it should have. I was to be tested even more during the next few weeks, but for now I was in my element and felt that I was invincible. Queen of the road, or so I imagined myself.

My stepfather was very unwell during this time and he unfortunately succumbed to his deteriorating health. He passed away one night, I got the news by a knock on the door and a policeman stood there asking if I could go back to look after my brother. Mother was being detained at the local police station as there were questions being asked. It fell to me to once again return home which took me about an hour and a half to get there. Mum's friend was holding the fort and my younger sister and I got there about a similar time. Apparently there was suspicion around the circumstances of his demise, and mother was under arrest. It fell to my sister and I to go to the police station to see what was going on. Mother's friend Georgina was prepared to stay with brother until we had more facts to go on. We were shown into the interview room where mum was being held.

We had a stern young policewoman to oversee us. Unfortunately our family had always had a 'gallows' humour and after asking mum what had happened we relapsed into seeing the funny side of the situation. My sister and I were joking about breaking her out and what flavour cake she wanted around the file and other daft things like that. The young WPC got annoyed with us and tried to impress on us the seriousness of the case. Although we knew mum was not really a caring type, we could not consider that she had actually murdered her husband, so expected it all to be sorted out and put down to a misunderstanding. With statements taken from both of us siblings, it was about eight o'clock the next morning when mother was eventually released to go home. Sis and I stayed for about another day ensuring that brother was okay, then we left and went back to our own homes.

The upshot of this meant that our stepfather needed a funeral. He had hoped to be buried back in Denmark in the family plot at Fåreveijle – mum decided this was too expensive – cremation was the next best thing. She organised this and booked a holiday to Denmark and liaised with the church there to bury the ashes in the family plot. This was the plan of the day, but necessitated driving to Denmark and she had lost her licence by then and had no transport. I was in the process of buying my first car, a BMW 2000 tilux so it fell to me to provide chauffeur service. Having organised a sitter for our brother, mum, Georgina, my sister and I had the burden of carrying out the sombre task, with stepfather in his urn on the back shelf. Within a month of passing my test, I was now driving on the wrong side of the road in Denmark. The journey was strange as sister and I were not really sympathetic with mother, Georgina thankfully was there to support mother and we were glad for that.

As soon as stepfather's ashes were interred it appeared business as usual as we then headed to Copenhagen, calling in on my older sister Kathy which did not please her. She had a one bedroom flat, and mum had expected her to let us stop for a week. This was despite mother leaving her alone in Copenhagen at the age of 16 when the rest of the family moved to Tenerife. Kathy was pleased to see our younger sister and me, so gave us her phone number so we could catch up another time. Mum decided to book us into a small hotel and got ready for party time. Rather than being a grieving widow, mother was treating this as one long joyride and holiday. She caught up with several old drinking buddies and was having a whale of a time. We were thrown together in an unwieldly bunch, tagging along in mother's wake. She booked up to see a couple of shows, and after one show when we had gone back to the hotel, my sister and I had to lock mother in her room as she was determined to go out clubbing at two o'clock in the morning. We were both aghast at her, but prevailed against her actions. Mother was definitely a wild child of the sixties – we used to call her the old age delinquent pensioner. She was always a nightmare, and by this time we had all just about had enough of her.

The journey home was even more eventful as she became ever more disgraceful. I felt like the party pooper as we had to restrain her worst extravagances. The first problem engineered by mother was when she practically kidnapped two young hitchhiking chaps who were touring Europe from Canada. The two lads had spent the previous night at the bar with mum and had the dubious pleasure of being invited to go home with her for a couple of days before seeing the rest of Britain. By the time we were disembarking from the boat she had persuaded them, and they were duly crammed into my car and brought home with mum. She entertained them, wined and dined them and was fully enjoying herself as a merry widow. She kept them for a fortnight before they escaped to resume their tour.

The other problem occurring on the boat home, was we discovered that during her visits to her friends she had acquired a carrier bag of 'grass', and a handbag full of seeds to grow more. I was mortified as I was the driver, at 20 years old the authorities would never believe a biker chic (wearing a leather jacket) like me to be innocent, while mother would be looked on as the well-dressed fifty year old woman of substance. I was in terror of my freedom being taken from me by her actions, but she was ever oblivious of anyone else's problems. She was an impossible parent. If ever daughters were beleaguered by a challenging parent, we felt we had drawn the short straw. The only good side to this trip was that we were almost home and my sister and I could get away, so long as we got through customs. I was bricking it for this bit, but despite the customs officer putting his head through mother's window somehow he did not smell – or recognise – the offending waft emanating from the baggage at her feet – he waved us through the Green Lane. My relief was enormous.

Having lived in the town for about four years Mum had established herself as a 'character' amongst the party set in the area. For most of the inhabitants she was full of fun and crazy ideas, but when related to her it was more excruciating. It definitely didn't seem fair to me that as a biker I was considered bad company, but mother smoked (anything and everything), drank to excess, extremely toxic towards other women (competition) and generally disruptive and often the cause of arguments with her peers (which included a few generations either side of hers) and appeared to be accepted. In my book another old Norfolk saying applied to her 'Ain't nowt so queer as folk'.

Once back in Norwich, I no longer felt comfortable driving my lovely BMW as every time I looked in my rear view mirror, I could not help but remember my stepfather's urn on the back shelf. I also decided that it was a bit expensive to run compared to my motorbike. Although happy with my factory work, the position I had was not long term as it was a seasonal food factory. I needed to find something else. I went for an interview for an insurance salesperson. It sounded interesting so I phoned up and got an interview. I arrived on time, waited in line with several other interviewees until I was called into the office. It started out well, until I was asked about my interests and did I drive. As per usual I got talking, waxing so lyrical about my car which I was having to sell. I told the man about my precious car and how I wanted it to go to a good home etc. This ended with me selling my car to the interviewer, sight unseen, and walked out with a cheque there and then. I was pleased as I had made a little profit on it. The funniest bit was having to make another appointment to find out what the job entailed. I went back the next day, gave the man the car log book and he said I could have the job as I could obviously sell. After going through the details, I declined as it involved a lot of evening and weekend appointments with customers, and those times were my precious social hours. With the money from the car I had a better bank balance to tide me over for the moment.

As I spent more time with Tina and John we had loads of good times. Tina and I decided we both needed new clothes so went into the city together. While shopping we both found and bought fairly skin tight denim catsuits. They were figure hugging and we both were lucky enough to have good slim figures, we looked and felt great which was quite unusual for us as we didn't often dress 'up'. I felt like a more comfortable version of Suzi Quatro in her leather one piece stage version, wearing it as my motorcycle clothing, usually with the legs tucked into my black cowboy boots. We both wore them a lot, and we felt they looked especially good when we went stock car racing with her husband. He raced and we were registered as his mechanics. There were several of his rivals who often tried to wind him up, saying that 'what is the good of having girls as mechanics? Adding 'they would be useless if something went wrong and he needed work done on his car!'

Tina and I were both grease monkeys and when the inevitable problem did occur, and John was towed out of the race track we popped the bonnet together, while John stomped off in a bit of a tizz. Knowing the looks we got from the disparaging other drivers, we cheerfully raided John's toolkits, and promptly started taking the head off the engine, hoping it was just a gasket which we could fix and get him back for the later races. Unfortunately it was not that simple, and appeared to be busted piston rings, but at least we had the last laugh as we obviously had ability which our looks concealed. John never got teased again about having useless 'mechanics'. I just loved the confused looks when I could be seen to be more than just a 'wannabe'.

Chapter 12 (21 – and Going Up in The World)

My bedsit was not ideal but living alone and not having to share my space with anyone else was liberating. Not having to compromise in order to do what I chose, the ability to go out without having to check whether it aligned with what someone else intended doing gave me opportunity to really start living my own life. I began going around in different social areas, and meeting a lot of new people. There were a lot of pubs in and around the Norwich area and joining in was easy. I was always chatty and friendly, becoming accepted into new groups without much trouble. Dating was fun and enjoyable – going out for meals, dances, car and motorcycle events, visiting friends – there was always something to do or somewhere to go – I did do and go all over the place.

I quickly got back to my own life and was a true petrol head now. I even got myself a job in a local scrap yard as a motorcycle messenger, but this also gave me the opportunity to borrow a car whenever I needed one. My boss not only owned the scrapyard, but also rented a few cars out. This was very helpful and I decided to go down to see my grandmother again, but this time I would go in a car so that I could take her out for a drive. I also wanted to take my little brother with me as he had not met his nan since he was about two years old. he was now nearly seven. My boss promised to let me have a Cortina MkIII which would be ready for me on the Friday at noon. I collected my brother by motorbike the evening before so we had an easy morning and walked to the yard to collect the car. We had to wait a couple of hours as the earlier renter was late bringing it back, but we eventually got the car, collected our bags from the bedsit and off we went. My brother was excited as I told him we would have a quick detour through London so he could see some of the important sights and buildings of our capital city. He was obsessed with London Bridge, I think because of the Nursery Rhyme and he wanted to see if there was still any signs of fire damage. I was able to show him the Tower of London and Westminster Palace before heading for the bridge, where brother got a closer look then he expected.

As ever, things never seem to go quite right for me, and we duly started to cross Tower Bridge. We had just gone under the first tower, the car broke down, we were holding up the London traffic. This was the mid-1970s and no mobile phones. There was only one thing for it, pop the bonnet and have a look. With no tool kit to hand, I grabbed my bag to see what I had that might help. I sacrificed my hairbrush and managed to 'sweep' the fur off the battery terminals, inexplicably I had a pair of pliers in my bag, so I tightened the terminals, gave the battery a knock. Looking about at the wires I pushed a couple together to make sure the connections I could see were all in place and secured them using both a phillips and flat screwdriver (which all good biker girls carry in their handbags). I put the bonnet down having done all I could and turned the key. Not having any idea of what the problem had been the car miraculously fired up and we were able to carry on with our journey. My little brother was awestruck that I had 'fixed' the car by myself and he remembered this escapade for years to come. We crossed back over to the north side of the Thames and drove by Buckingham Palace before heading west to catch the M3 then A303 and dropping down to Salisbury and Fordingbridge.

By the time we had stopped for a bite to eat, we finally arrived in Hampshire but it was a bit late to turn up at nan's, we parked up and slept in the car until morning. Brother was really enjoying his mini holiday and it was an adventure for him. On waking we went to the local shop and bought bacon, sausages, mushrooms, eggs and bread for a good fry-up as I knew we were hungry. Nan was surprised to see us but pleased, especially when I cooked a lovely British breakfast for us all as she got to know her grandson. We stayed for the night taking nan out for a roast meal on the Sunday, before heading home to Norfolk. That morning brother and I had hidden money around her flat before taking nan out for our lunch. This was something I always did when visiting her, I would have a load of change to hide around her flat –she knew I would do this – leaving nan to have a bit of fun spending some time having a mini treasure hunt after we left. We dropped nan off at her door after lunch and drove off, knowing that for days to come she would find coins in unexpected places. The reason I would do this was to take her mind off worrying about our drive home.

One of the guys I saw for a while was a larger than life character. Charlie had a Kawasaki Z900 which had been adapted with a Rickman nose fairing and a set of clip-on handlebars. We met up several times while on our respective bikes, but one night we were going to an event a few miles out from the city. Unusually I chose to go on the back of Charlie which turned out a bit hair-raising. Having normally been on my own machine I had not realised quite how much of a drinker he was. During the evening he consumed far more alcohol than he should have and I did not want to go home on the pillion. With no other option than to ride home with Charlie, I appropriated the keys, put him on the back and rode him home. This idea was fine in principle, but I was not quite eight stone in weight (about 50 kg) and Charlie was over thirteen stones (about 90 kg) but this should not have been a problem. It would not have been a problem at all on a standard bike, but it was not easy with clip-on handlebars. The second problem was that on the way home Charlie was drunk and his head was higher than mine. Every bend we got to, he tried to steer the bike by leaning with his weight. By the time we had got back to Charlie's house my nerves were fraught, relieved to have got back in one piece it gave me the confidence to believe in myself once more. If I had managed to ride a Z1 with a drunken mass wobbling about behind me while riding in an unnatural position over the tank, then I realised I could ride a Z1 if I could get one of my own. To be at the mercy of a drunken companion was not my idea of fun so I made the resolution to stay single for the time being.

Knowing that riding the Z1 had been well within my abilities, the new target in my life was to get my own, so I set about working out the plan to acquire one. I had now had my Z400 for nearly two years and felt that I had the experience to go large. Once again I visited the bike shop in Lowestoft where I had bought my Z400 and found the Z1 had been uprated to a Z1000 – there in the showroom was my dream – a turquoise green beautiful machine – waiting for me. The updates included double front disc brake and a rear disc brake, which I was now used to braking with, they were meant to be better than the drum rear which the Z1s had mostly been fitted with. The bike had also had several modifications to the frame and Avon had designed a new tyre called a Red Arrow which had been modelled around the Z1 – the effect of this was to more or less eradicate the tank slapper which was supposed to affect the handling of the earlier models. I was curious and took the brochures home to read up on it all. I was enamoured with the new model and decided there and then I had to have one.

Together with my savings and my Z400 I had over a third of the value of the Z1000 and I had to find a further £1000 to be able to bring this prize home. I went to the bank to find out how much a loan would cost and decided I could afford it, but as I was not quite 21 I wasn't deemed old enough to be allowed a loan without a guarantor. Stumbling at this hurdle was a nuisance as I obviously did not have any back up from a parent or relative. I was a bit disheartened wondering how I could raise the money. When talking to one of the chaps in my new circle of mates he offered me a private loan, saying I could pay him back the equivalent to the bank's calculations. I knew he was a wealthy man and he was able to afford this so I took him up on his offer. He said that he would get more interest on his investment than if he kept the money in the bank so the deal was made and he came to the bike shop to see the bike I was buying. He was a bit surprised at the size of the bike, but he happily wrote a cheque and the bike was bought – I was to pick it up for my 21st birthday present to myself. I felt I needed something to look forward to, and to restart my life on a new track, well this was it, I was so proud of my gleaming new motorbike.

If I hadn't already got enough self-confidence then the next month boosted it skywards. The weather took a turn for the worse, the heavens opened and we got several weeks of snow. My bike was my only transport, so not only was I getting used to a larger bike – the basic weight was five times my weight – it was one of the biggest bikes available at that time. I had to learn quickly how to keep upright and I was lucky not to have any major accidents. On one downhill country road I very nearly came a cropper, the bike slalomed its way down to a T-junction, it slipped to the left, then to the right and back to the left. I thought I was going to drop it but miraculously held it by the time I got to the bottom. After this near miss my ego went through the roof and I felt invincible – the bike would look after me. As the weather got better, my head grew simultaneously and I knew no fear whilst riding around the county. The only obstacle I had to jump now was that my bedsit did not offer parking and I was reluctant to park on the street, albeit with a couple of heavy chains to deter thieves.

I started looking at the classified adverts in the local paper for somewhere else to live. It seemed to be a lot cheaper to rent somewhere out of the city and I made a short-list of a few properties which appeared to be in my price range. Some were no better than where I was and did not have any safe parking, others were really not right for other reasons. After a couple of weeks of looking around I saw an advert for a small place in one of the nearby market towns which sounded great, even having a garage and outbuilding. I rang the landlord and arranged to view it. One of my older friends came with me to lend me a mature support as I did not want my obvious youth to be a bar. I felt that this property was meant for me, and so it was. The cottage came fully furnished, ready to move in with my meagre belongings. The rent was only £10.00 more per month than my bedsit in Norwich. I was elated when the landlords decided they liked me and that I could have it. I paid the deposit there and then, and moved in the following weekend.

Chapter 13 Moving On, Have Bike, Will Travel

Having managed to secure the small cottage, I finally had a home of my own in a town just 10 miles from the city. I'd fallen in love with it immediately on that first viewing, and this feeling was not diminished upon moving in. It helpfully had a small garage, a workshop, small garden and a couple of stables. With my new motorbike and new home, I was again thinking life would fall into place at last. The cottage had three bedrooms so I had the chance to rent a room out to help with the rent if I needed. It was within walking distance to the shops and only 500 yards from the local biker pub. I had a job I loved at a garage, with a pick of vehicles for personal use. I really felt I was on my feet at last, and I was. In less than a year from leaving Chip I was self-sufficient, with everything I could wish for in my life. I was able to let my brother come over for a night or two, he absolutely loved coming out on my bike with me. It was inevitable that he would become a petrol head too.

After living in my cottage for a month I tentatively asked the landlady if she was happy for me to have a dog. She was cautious at first and asked what sort of dog would I get and what about work? I had already okayed it with my boss to take the dog to work with me, so she was happy that it wouldn't always be left for hours. It turned out that my landlady had a market stall to raise funds for an animal charity so she was not averse to dogs, so long as it didn't upset the neighbours. When I told her I wanted an Alsatian she was happy as that was her favourite breed too. I again looked to the classified ads to find myself a puppy. I found some in Norwich and went on my bike to look at the litter. There was a little female pup who immediately came to me, telling me she wanted to be mine, so money changed hands and she came home with me – tucked inside my jacket – and my family had started.

I called my little dog Jo, in memory of my childhood dog whom I had lost some six years beforehand. She was the perfect dog and with a bit of consistency became the most loving well behaved little girl. Everyone loved her sweet nature, she was quiet and friendly, too quiet so that I had to teach her to bark to order – she was meant to be a guard dog too so I needed a bit of assertion from her. Once she cottoned on to the bark duties all was well. I had to crouch down like a dog, knock on the door and pretend to bark until she learned to do it herself. We had such fun together, there was a park where I was able to walk her morning and evening just behind our row of cottages, I also had a panel taken out of the rear kitchen door for her to come and go into the garden at will. She practically house-trained herself and was no trouble. This was the most relaxed I had been in my life, I had it all and I was happy.

By the time she had been with me two months even my boss wanted to keep her. He was amazed that when I worked on the fuel pumps, Jo would either stay in her bed if I told her to, or she would wander out with me to serve the customers. When it got busy and it was safer for her to be inside in her bed I only had to point and tell her and at just four months old she would do as she was told. The customers were all good with her, she loved the fuss she got, people would come to our garage just to see her. I've never met a dog so good with people, even those who did not like dogs would sit in the garage and pet her. Just one of those character dogs I was proud to own. Or did she own me. She definitely owned my heart. Of course there were times I wanted to go out on my bike, and by then I was renting a spare room to a friend who would happily dog sit when I went out.

Georgina was actually my mother's friend, but they had fallen out and she needed somewhere to live. We settled into a comfortable time as Georgie got a part-time job and was happy to contribute towards the household bills. Although she was a couple of decades older than I was, we got on well, both being aquarians we had a whacky sense of humour, always joking and having fun. Nervous at first, she enjoyed coming out on the back of my bike and like me, she loved riding fairly quick. On the way out one day I was riding a bit quick with her on the back. Enjoying ourselves was infectious and I was overtaking a line of cars, obviously speeding up to return to my own side of the road when we passed a police car going in the opposite direction. Oh no. damn. I saw him turn around in the distance behind us, and sure enough, on came the blue lights. I did think about gunning it, but realised that he could radio ahead, I slowed down to 60 mph (the limit there) and he caught up with us and flagged me down. I stopped in a layby and the policeman pulled in front of me. Georgie and I duly got off and stood beside the bike. The policeman was taken aback that I was a female rider, and after looking around the bike to check for defaults – which there obviously weren't any, it was only a few months old – he proceeded to tell me off. While he was lecturing me, with 'most lads when they get a bike this big, they have usually acquired some sense,' but all he could do was give me a ticket as he had been unable to accurately record my speed. I was mumbling the normal, yes officer, no officer, sorry officer, I won't do it again officer, trying my best to be believable. He was interrupted by a disruption and squeal for help, smothered by giggling. Georgie, finding the event hilarious, had laughed so much to see me being all penitent, she had fallen into the ditch beside us. The policeman helped me pull her up, shook his head, gave me a 'producer' and with a last bit of stern advice let us go. Once out of sight, Georgie and I fell about until we were capable of carrying on with our ride.

Borrowing a car one Thursday, I determined it was time to introduce Jo to the landlords. She was by now four months old and at the height of cuteness, so I deemed it to be a good time for the introductions. We went to the market town where they had their stall so that made it easy to just turn up. Being dog lovers, they took to Jo and were reassured that I was a responsible dog owner. They were happily impressed with Jo's manners and that even so young she did not need to be on a lead. Being used to people at the garage and coming round to our home, she was completely at ease, and totally unflappable. Georgie had come with me for the drive and I was glad that Jo and Georgie had both been approved of.

Of course, like any animal lover, having a dog did not end there. I was out one day, visiting a farm where they had a litter of kittens, I could not choose whether to have the black and white one, or the pretty little tabby. Of course, it had to be both, and they were duly paid for and popped into the pet friendly jacket and whisked home on the motorbike. The kittens had already been familiar with the farm dogs so I was sure they would be fine with Jo, and she was so loving I knew she would take to the kittens. Sammy and Tiger fitted in as though an Alsatian was a normal sister to have. All three used to cuddle up together from the very first meeting. As the year progressed and it became necessary to have a fire on at night, Jo used to lay as close to the fireside as possible, and Tiger would lay on top of her so they both had the heat before any other inhabitants were allowed to feel it.

Eventually the homestead branched out into keeping a few ducks, they were housed in the stable area where I used a paddling pool for a small pond. They arrived one evening after a friend mentioned he had caught them on a duck pond in a nearby village. I don't know what had motivated the duck-napping, but they could not stay in the boot of his car so they got put in the stable for a few months. The reason for the delay in rehoming them elsewhere was because there was a dispute between us. He was feeding them – to fatten them up for eating – I obviously couldn't agree with that. By this time I had named them – you can't eat a pet – or let someone else eat them. The house pets were not in agreement either. Jo was happy to have them as friends, but the cats were not averse to duck tasting, they were just too small to actually catch them and the ducks were quite capable of pecking them back. It was an ill assorted menagerie so I had to make a decision. The three ducks were not small enough to go in my jacket and I had to borrow a van from work. I got hold of a couple of boxes from town and boxed them up. Taking them to the duck pond in the town I set them all free to interact with the wild ducks there.

My friend was a bit miffed, but I felt I had done my bit for conservation.

My social life now was centered around the biker pub just up the road. Jo was allowed in so it was my normal practice to take her for a walk first, then we would go to the pub for a drink where one of the old boys who went in there every night looked forward to having Jo beside him for an hour or two. Jo could hear the rattle of a packet of crisps from the far corners of a noisy pub and was there with him as soon as he opened a packet. The pub was happy for her to roam at will and I am sure she enjoyed the evenings as much as anyone else. There was nearly always several bikers frequenting the bar on any night of the week. I never drank alcohol but loved socializing with them all and I soon merged into the group. The first night I went down there was quite a laugh. I had been out to see a friend and popped in on my motorbike on my own. Most of the bikes were smaller than mine and I just parked up in the corner, took my helmet off and walked into the pub on my own.

As I walked into the crowded pub there was a bit of a hush as I obviously was a new face, unknown by the locals. I went up to the bar, grabbed a seat and ordered myself a coke. I got talking to a lad and gradually everyone restarted their conversations. After a few minutes it was obvious I was not 'with' someone and curiosity got the better of several of the boys. Ian, who I was talking to asked in conversation if I was meeting anyone. My answer that I was not, and was on my own, opened up more dialogue. Did I have my own bike then, as I had a helmet with me? Again, the answer was yes, I had my own bike. What did I have? A Kawasaki. Oh, nice. After about ten minutes Ian went to the loo, obviously went outside to look at the 'strange' bike and came in a bit shell-shocked. He came and sat beside me and asked, do you mean that Z1000 is yours? I obviously said yes. There was then a not so discreet coming and going of most of the rest of the lads as they went out to inspect my bike. Most of them didn't know what to say, so didn't say anything. A couple came up to me and were more direct in their questions, most assuming I was some rich kid and not a 'real' biker.

It took a few weeks but eventually the idea of a female riding a Z1000 became old news and for the most I was slowly integrating with the local population of bikers. Most of the bikers here were still riding older British bikes with their idiosyncrasies. Robert had a Norton Commando Hi-rider, which had a 750cc combat engine. This was a highly tuned engine and was a temperamental starter. I was stunned when I saw it as I had hoped to buy that particular motorcycle when it had been at Jeff Priest's motorbike shop in Norwich just over three years before. I had failed that first bike test, so I was not in a position to buy it then, and Jeff had sold it before I eventually got my bike licence. I was pleased to see it still on the road and was happily admiring it. The owner, Rob, came out and said that it was a good job I hadn't bought it as I would not be able to start it. I replied that of course I could, knowing I had already learned the secrets of old British bike techniques. He laughed and chucked me the key, "prove it," he taunted!

I duly put the key in the notch, tinkered with the kick start, raised myself when I had the cylinder just over top dead center – I balanced myself on top of the raised kick start, did a hop, skip and jump, landed with my full weight down onto the starter and swung the starter down. It started first kick, much to Rob's amazement. At first he said it must have been a fluke, but when I stopped and restarted the bike three times he acknowledged I could start it. He laughed and said that he had bought it cheaply from a mate who had it for about three years, but could never start it. My street cred went up a notch for that.

A few weeks later I finally fully passed muster when coming back from one of the villages, I was riding behind a couple of the boys when my headlights blew, both head and dip, it was a dark night and I did not know the road. The boys disappeared into the distance as the inevitable happened and I careered off the road at about 60 plus mph. I upended the bike into a ditch and flew through a bramble bush head first. I landed in a soft ploughed area. The boys ahead of me hadn't missed me at first, but when they realised I was not behind them they turned around to come look for me. Meanwhile, back in the ditch, I lay still, opened my eyes, and could not see anything. I didn't know if I was alive. I moved slowly, first my hands which I could feel, then my feet and gradually bit by bit, the rest of my body parts. I didn't seem to have hurt myself badly so I slowly stood up.

It was a pitch black night, so dark that I had to wait a few minutes before a car drove along the road so that I could see where the road was. I walked carefully in that direction before I heard the two motorbikes returning, looking for me. They both drove past me before realising that the person waving to them on the side of the road had to be me. After checking me over, they shone their lights towards the ditch and my top box was just visible. They left the bike illuminated as they helped to pull it out of the ditch and back to the road. We checked it over, the engine crash bars had limited much of the potential damage, but my handlebars were at a funny angle, one bar about five inches higher than the other one. Luckily the ignition key was still in the lock so I switched it back on, all control lights showing, good. I then turned it to see if it would start, it did. Okay, rear lights ok but no front ones. The boys said they could get the bike collected the following day if I wanted a lift back to town. I said no, one of you ride ahead, the other behind, I'll ride in between the two of you and sort the repairs the next morning.

After that crash I was deemed to be one of the lads as was my usual place in the biker world, especially as I obviously did not have some sort of sugar daddy there to pick up the pieces. I was accepted as 'one of them' and a lot of the reserve I had experienced up until that occasion disappeared. Fortunately the biggest cost to this incident was a pair of new handlebars which I bought and I was allowed to go down the workshop which the lads shared at a local farm. It was not quite straightforward but with the help of a Haynes manual we prevailed. The wiring for the bars were routed internally in the handlebars so it was a bit fiddly but do-able. My leather jacket had upside down bramble tears back and front, my helmet had a few scratches but I survived, wearing my scratches like a badge of passage. The engine crash bars I'd had fitted when buying the bike had saved the bike from being badly damaged. This was my third accident and I felt myself lucky to not have had any serious injuries. I had been let off lightly again.

Chapter 14 Z1 and Holidays For All

I was ready for another adventure now, and what could be better than to take my beautiful Z1000 to the Isle of Man. I was thinking about going on my own and spoke about going while at the pub. Someone said that a few of the lads were going, and I ought to talk about going with them, or at least travelling with them. I thought that sounded a good idea and asked around to find out who was going. The lads who were planning their trip did not always come into town so I had to wait a couple of weeks to catch up with them, to see if they would be happy if I tagged along with them. They were happy to do so as the more the merrier was their attitude. They said they were meeting up at a pub outside of town on the next Sunday if I wanted to go talk to the whole group.

I was quite excited about the prospect of joining them on the road as it is more fun to be a part of a group, even though I was quite happy to go it alone. It turned out that none of them had been before, so they were more than keen for me to ride with them as I knew where to go. One of the lads caught my eye and we palled up as he did not live far from me. The other lads all lived in the surrounding villages. My new mate was friendly and ended up coming into the pub a bit more. We talked about the trip and the fact that the boys had booked a three bedroomed flat in Douglas for the two weeks. He would talk with the boys to see if they were prepared to double up a bit so that I could have a room to myself in the flat. This seemed a great idea to me, and saved me having to find my own accommodation. I only had to buy a ticket for the ferry and I was on the point of ordering one when one of the lads had a problem and was not able to go. Would I like his ferry ticket.

Would I? Of course I would, it would mean I didn't have to worry about getting a different ferry to the others. I found a local pet kennels for the girls, and all was set for the trip. It was all falling into place.

My house became a convenient coffee stop and I found more and more of my new circle of friends were popping in on me. I have always loved being social, having friends around and a new routine opened up as most of the lads loved my dog, several of the girls started coming round too as it was more relaxed for those still living at home with parents. I felt that I belonged at last and this was one of the happiest periods of my life so far. No-one to answer to, mistress of my own destiny, mother of my own pets and captain of my life. With the holiday looming my house quickly filled up with friends, all just starting out on our lives, filling them with plans and ideas. Several of the lads had started building their own custom bikes and the fact that I had a garage with a workshop too meant a gravitation of lads. Alex had become more of a friend by now, he was a gifted engineer along with his mate Rodger, the two of them by now had more or less taken over the workshop, both of them were engineers and worked well together. Within the group of bikers there was a wealth of mechanical talent and my workshop became a central hub for the lads.

As I was the only one of us who had my own home, it was decided that we would all meet up at mine on the evening before setting off for my beloved Isle of Man. All the bikes were to be brought round the night before riding off, with baggage loaded up ready, the lads were driven home by one of them in his car and he was going to pick them all up in the morning so that they would not be waiting around for anyone. All sorted, my new pal was staying with me in order to avoid disturbing his parents as we were setting off early. There were eight of us all travelling up together, six were sharing the flat (including myself) two of the boys were camping, and we were meeting up with a brother on the way to Liverpool as he was coming from Tyneside. It looked as though Alex was becoming my new companion too, as we got closer over the months we had known each other. I couldn't wait to go back to my dream holiday destination.

The journey to Liverpool was really enjoyable for me, as mostly I rode on my own. I was either commuting, or going to visit friends. It was good to think of a companiable biker trip. I had written out the waypoints for everyone to have on their tanks in case they went astray on route, but as we were keeping to the main roads this was as a precaution only. I had outlined fuel stops for roughly 100 mile gaps which was a residue memory from my earlier Italian trip. This was a minimum for comfort, and enabled us to stretch our legs and knees for a few minutes. The reality was that we stopped at 50 mile intervals for the smokers amongst us. Apparently their lungs needed to be fumigated. In those days most people smoked, which was another way I was always the odd one out. I would more often find somewhere to lay down and doze if the weather was warm and dry enough. They all used to laugh at me, saying that I would sleep through a major catastrophe.

We met up with our mates brother at the services on the M6 and rode the rest of the way to Liverpool. The lads were astounded by the sheer number of motorbikes all waiting in the old dry dock sheds. Thousands and thousands of bikers, all waiting for the boats on a first come first served basis. Luckily the days of being craned on and off the boats seemed to have stopped and the ferries were all ride on vehicle ferries. Nevertheless, we had to wait out for about the fourth boat before our turn came to board. Along with the thousands of peers, we embarked, tied our bikes in rows across the deck and hurried to find an area to rest in. We took turns to go on deck and watch as we left the docks and got on our way, the next need was to get to the restaurant for something to eat while our mates looked after our hand luggage and helmets. Finally, as the trip settled we laid out as best we could on the benches and floors to get some much needed rest. We were nearly there, only four hours of rhythmic dozing before arriving at Douglas.

Once we were installed in our flat, we were pleased as we had a good view and could see the sea, the downside was we were on the third floor, with no lift. I made sure the lads did not think that as I was the girl I should do the shopping and cooking. No, it was my holiday too and I was not going to be a drudge. Stereotypes out the window. We had a discussion about chores and it was agreed that we couldn't all do everything, so it was decided that we should have some sort of rote. As I was used to housekeeping, and to make sure we didn't forget anything I agreed to coordinate the shopping more or less every day, but all other chores like cooking and washing up was theirs. Also, I would go shopping, but I had to have at least one other lad with me to carry the heavier items home. Fair enough – we all agreed – and put £50.00 each into a food fund, to be topped up if necessary as we went on.

For the first shop it was natural by then for myself and Alex to go, and another of the lads came with us as this was going to be the biggest session. The boys all took turns after that until it got to Tim's turn. Anyway, Tim was to shop with me that day, but he was not a natural at pitching in and was very grumpy as he followed me around the shops. He was outraged that I expected him to carry the bags, moaning that he had not come on holiday to act as a porter, blah, blah. He annoyed me as the other lads had all been quite happy to go along with the agreed rote tasks. Due to Tim's belligerence I reciprocated and decided that would be the day I bought potatoes and cans of vegetables. This enraged Tim and by the time we walked home, he was furious with me. As we got back to the apartment he was at boiling point, the boys could hear him as we approached the flat. Mick came down to help, but by then the pot spilled over and Tim ascended the stairs, absolutely stomping loudly on each tread, swearing as he landed on each individual stair as he went up the entire three floors. Mick and I collapsed with laughter, tears streaming from our eyes as we heard the fracas. Within the choice but varied words emitting from our friend, I got called all manner of things, but the one that stuck was me being referred to as the 'Majorette' – Alex was a prominent character within the group and a few of the lads had nicknamed him 'the Major'. I got an apology the next day from Tim, but the laugh we all got out of his outburst was payment enough.

The island was all I remembered and was thoroughly enjoyed by all of us. I won't repeat my personal thrills here as my first book (Manners, Morals & Motorbikes) covered the Isle of Man extensively, but suffice to say I did take the lads to Gooseneck for viewing during racing – more than just once – but in general we rode together with occasional splitting up into sub groups. It was very much up to each of us to decide where we wanted to go, chatting in the morning and going wherever the fancy took us. The boys did not have the appetite for revisiting my favourite cafes for Apple Pie and Ice Cream, but I found the quality still worth the re-tastings. We did many of the 'must view' places like the Fairy Bridge, The Chasms in the south and the iconic Laxey Wheel which had to be climbed up.

During our trip to Laxey, I wanted to check if the café was still producing good apple pie with cream. We parked up at the car park near the beach and had the first sight of two experimental enclosed motorbikes. The machines were prototypes and looked like mini space ships. They were silver and very futuristic, looking almost like a two wheeled DeLorean, complete with front screen, roof and usable lockable boot. Designed and built by two friends in Devizes, Wiltshire originally with Reliant Robin engine. They were called a Quasar and were like nothing we had seen before, and rarely since. I believe there were only about 20 original bikes, but had a few re-incarnations using many various bike engines to power them, possibly under a hundred bikes in total. The chaps riding these two were delighted with their rides, surprising us with their views on the handling and the speed of these vehicles, cruising around 90mph, top speed in the region of 100 mph. I don't know why they were never put into full production because in my opinion they were a great compromise if you needed an all year commuter bike. They were ahead of their time, and should have been put into manufacture, at least around the release of 'Back to the Future'.

The aim of our holiday was the racing and we watched from various viewpoints. One of the highlights for me came during the senior race – looking forward to seeing the legendary Mike Hailwood – my absolute favorite IOM rider – make a comeback race after several years away from the track. Also making a return was Phil Read – Tim's hero. Always up for a bit of fun, this was too good to miss baiting Tim again. I had been pronouncing Mike as the best rider ever, to the point where Tim told me to put my money where my mouth was. A bet was made between us, witnessed by the rest of the group. We sat at Braddan Bridge where the local church kindly provided pews and seats in the graveyard overlooking the double bend. There was also a cake and sandwich facility, so a first class view point. We all sat together for this race, and were beside ourselves as Hailwood and Read were getting closer and closer on the road. The staggered starts meant that Hailwood was behind Read for the first couple of laps, but joy, oh joy. On the last lap, as they approached the bend Phil Rad came round the left hander, but Hailwood was hot on his heels, and just cruised past Phil leaving him behind by the time they got to the righthand bend and disappeared out of sight. Phil was hanging off his bike as he used to, obviously doing his utmost to win, but Mike rode around him nonchalantly, almost as though he was on a Sunday afternoon pleasure jaunt. Tim couldn't contain his annoyance and refused to pay up. It was only a small token bet so I was not really bothered, I was elated to have my hero come out tops proving me right.

Even if you don't want to see the racing, there is always so many things to see and do. We wanted to do something different so went off to explore the railways, taking the steam train from Douglas – near the ferry terminal – down to Castletown and Port Erin. This train was first used in the early 1870s, runs on a narrow gauge for about 15 miles, and is still using much of its original rolling stock. After this train we took the horse trams to the northern end of Douglas seafront, where the electric train started its journey to Laxey where it is possible to change trains for the mountain section, going up to the Bungalow and thereafter to the summit of Snaefell. On the way back towards Douglas we saw some great coastline which looked interesting, necessitating a bit of exploring.

The next day we rode down a couple of small tracks and found a great little bay not far from Douglas, a few of the lads spent some happy hours handline fishing from the rocks, catching mostly catfish. I would have loved to have swum, but revised this opinion as soon as my toes hit the freezing water, also put off by the first catches proudly displayed. The two weeks flew by, the weather was absolutely hot. We had wanted to swim but on the day picked it ended up raining, ever the optimists we still decided to head the other side of the mountain and finished up at Ramsey. Having gone the other side of the central ridge which often divided the weather, it was now hot and sunny again. We had not brought our swimwear so we did a spot of skinny dipping, the sea looking so inviting. Yes, the water was still very cold, but with the sun so hot it was fun to cool off.

Finally we found the other railway which was the clifftop Douglas Head Funicular Railway, this took passengers up the steep 60° incline from the seafront esplanade to the Cliff Hotel. Built originally in 1927 it was actually the second railway to serve the hotel at the top, but the earlier one was on a different site to the final 'lift' which closed around 1990, the car ran on a 5ft (1524mm) gauge for about 40 metres and was wobbly as it ascended, giving views out over Douglas Bay as it rose up the steep cliffside. Sadly this icon of our rail history fell into disrepair, probably still giving room for abundant vegetation to date, last seen disappearing under the brambles.

All too soon the holiday used up its days and it was time to come home. We were exhausted and all felt we needed another one to get over it. 14 days in the open air, climbing and clambering over hill and dale will take the stuffing out of even the best of us. The boat home was a bit of an anticlimax and we rode home subdued with the thought of back to work. The bright side of my return was to pick up my pets, Sam, Tiger and especially Jo. They were all pleased to see me, and the funny side of Jo's kennel trip was the owners husband. When I had first gone to look at the kennels to make sure they were suitable for my girls, the husband was cleaning one of the exercise areas. I spoke to him and he asked what sort of dog I was intending to bring in. When I told him I had an Alsatian he was dubious and said he didn't really like them as he didn't trust them. I said he would love my Jo. This proved to be the case and he had apparently taken him with him out in the car several times and she hardly left his side for the whole fortnight. He came and saw me when I collected her and told me he was sad to see her go home because she was so loving and friendly. I often wonder whether he still thinks of her.

Back to playing house and in my happy state as Mrs Noah (owner of Noah's Ark) one of my friends came round with a small black stray kitten. She had found it wandering, mewing pitifully and her parents would not let her keep it. The thought struck her that I would like it, so she duly presented herself with the bundle of hissing, spitting fur ball. Although not really intending to have any more pets, I could not say no. We found a small box and kitted it out so it was warm and comfy. The little feline was very small, probably only about four weeks old, I was not sure if it could lap yet. I found an old dropper medicine dispenser, cleaned it out and filled it with milk. The kitten was extremely hungry and couldn't get it down quick enough. Once fed and feeling more relaxed I put it in a corner of the dining room so it could sleep quietly. Poor little thing.

When I heard it mewing again, I collected it up, fed it again and introduced it to Tiger and Sam who were not sure at first, but slowly sniffed and introduced themselves to it. The next thing I knew was, they all cuddled up together and the little brother joined our family. Jo was never going to have an issue with it, and nor did she. Once it realised it was being fed, watered and had a home it settled in without a backward glance. Alex was more of a dog lover and was not keen on another cat arriving, but that was not for him to decide. Although never cruel to this newcomer he did not encourage it. Bit of a mistake. Panther as I named him grew and grew, until he was a beautiful sleek adult. His figure was athletic, like a Siamese, and he held himself majestically at all times. The trouble was that he had the most enormous bright yellow eyes.

Alex found this alarming as invariably when we came indoors to watch a bit of TV, when the telly was on it got warm, and obviously was the best place in the world to a lazy black male cat. Panther would spread out on his viewing platform, and would proceed to stare at Alex, Rodger or Stan if they were in the room. They all found it impossible to concentrate on the program as their eyes would be drawn to the big yellow eyes staring back at them, just above the screen. Set in a black face they were mesmerising, but apparently disconcerting to the boys. There was a standoff as all thought they were the top of the chain, but the cat would have the last laugh as it drove them out, the cat unnerved them every time. The difference when I came in the room was that I was a more comfortable lap, with a petting and stroking service provided, he would happily come to snuggle up with me.

Feeling a bit deflated after the IOM, and another year before the prospect of a return tour it was back to the routine of daily life. But who could be down with life when it seems to be providing all I could want. With a spare room available, I found the number I had been given the previous year and phoned my older sister who had been left in Denmark about nine years before. I invited her to come over and stay anytime she felt like it. To my delight, she phoned back a few weeks later telling me she was on her way. I was now 21, she was 24, and we hadn't really seen each other since I was 13 and she 16. We hadn't known each other as adults. I said I could meet her which I did, borrowing Alex's GT6. It was an emotional reunion, she couldn't believe how much I was grown, and that I could drive a car. As she had been living in Copenhagen for the last decade she had never thought about having a vehicle of her own, there was always buses and trains. When she saw I also had my own home, and that she could come back anytime she was overcome. She had missed having family around, but was not prepared to live with mother again, for reasons which I fully understood. She did a lot of thinking, and decided she would like to come back to England to live, and get to know not just me but our younger sister too. She wasn't sure because she did not have much money to relocate, but I reassured her that my house was her house, she could come and stay with me forever, if she wished.

The upshot of this was she went back to Copenhagen, gave her job up to move home and country. Georgie had by this time already moved to be with her eldest daughter who had not long had her first baby. Having Kathy come back was great, and we went all over the county on my bike. This opened up her thoughts and she decided it would be good to have her own transport. As she had had a moped for a time until it had been stolen, she was sure she could manage my bike and that I could teach her on it. I was horrified as this was not the ideal learner bike. It took a lot of persuading, until Alex heard of a friend selling a Suzuki 185. Thankfully it was not a lot of monies and I saved my precious Z1000 from potential woman handling, I sacrificed my savings and we now had a machine suitable for her.

Between the four of us, me, Alex, Stan and Rodger, we all took turns to ride pillion and teach her the controls and survival skills, but also logistics of the local area as we mentored her. It was not long before she too passed her bike test and graduated to a Honda XL250. For longer outings she would still come on the back of me, but she really came alive with her newfound independence. We lived, rode, shopped, laughed and generally we were both overjoyed to have each other around. It had been a low point in her life when I had phoned her out of the blue, but it was the best thing for both of us.

Everything that I had been able to build up was the tonic she needed, and to have her sisters close meant a lot to her. She was one of the funniest natural comics I have ever been blessed to have in my life, but she never realised how funny she was. It was like living with a cross between a female Mr Bean and Frank Spencer, before they ever televised the concept. Having lived abroad for the formative years of her life, she did not quite understand the more 'prudish' ways and 'stiff upper lip' of the British was inconceivable to her. She was to the point, brash and brutally honest, at all times. Often we were reduced to tears of laughter while she stood there, not understanding, asking what we were laughing at? How do you tell someone, we're laughing at you?

She never understood why we were laughing, but she would just take the cue, laugh in an infectious way which set us all off again, into a spiral of belly aching hilarity. The stitches I incurred in my sides, just being with her, was uplifting to the top degree, and I miss her so much. She eventually studied as a nurse and joined the renal unit in Norwich, with her natural comic ways she worked her magic, with many a patient asking her to go away because laughing with her was hurting them while they were having their bloods sucked out of them. They say laughter is the best medicine and her colleagues all confirmed – with her on the ward they knew they would have a good shift, however hard the work was.

Chapter 15 Projects and Happy Days

A ll through the sixties and seventies bikers were always looking for ways to individualize their motorcycles. The prevailing style was the café racer epitomized by aluminium tanks and clip on handlebars. In Norfolk there were so many engineering workshops and factories that many young lads had learned the skills to formulate their own parts for their bikes. There was also a market which arose so that for those less accomplished they could look at and buy from catalogues or magazine adverts. The variety of bolt on pieces had built an aftermarket trade of its own and by the late seventies and early eighties the choice was burgeoning. There were a few motorcycle shows starting to become popular, most at this time were in London and were held during the winter months – the main 'building' months. As the summer died down, and the boys thoughts went to major rebuilds or revamps of their bikes, a couple of the lads decided to go down to the Racing and Sporting Show at the Royal Horticultural Halls in Lambeth. As ever, the discussions in the pub attracted other like-minded lads and when they got together over a pint they thought it would be nice to make a trip of it. Helen and her husband had a Bedford Minibus/Van and offered to take a group of eight if anyone wanted to join them. Alex and I, and a few others all put our names down and the trip was agreed.

As usual, my cottage was the starting point and a time of 6.30am agreed as the meeting time. I have never been an early riser, but for events and excitement am happy to see the world, but am never really awake until a few hours after the country early hours brigade. As per usual I got up in a blur, was installed at the back of the van and as we set off, I happily fell back asleep. The trip went without mishap until we hit London. The boys had not really driven much outside of our own county and it wasn't long before a couple of wrong turns and we were completely lost. Having driven around some sort of housing estate for about half an hour and not getting anywhere recognisable, Alex sat in the front and said, 'we better wake HER up'. The lads all asked, 'Why? Does she know her way around here? Alex replied, 'I don't know, but she can normally find where she wants to go'. Apparently they all looked unsure, not wanting to disturb a sleeping dog. Helen gently roused me, and told me they were lost, could I help? I rubbed my eyes, sleepily got into the front bench seat. I looked about and apart from a couple of tower blocks the housing all looked the same. I just said drive a bit so I can get my bearings. Helpfully London would put the first part of the postcode on the road signs, so I worked out quickly we were in the North East of London. As we came to a T-junction I saw that most of the cars were parked heading to our right, so told Paul to turn left. (I figured people would drive into the estate and park in the direction they were travelling). As we came to a few adjoining roads, I just said to go slowly so I could work out where to go next. As the parked cars direction changed I looked into adjoining roads and spotted the cars looking our way and turned into those roads. The boys were all asking me how did

I know where I was? In my usual way I left them wondering. After about ten minutes we picked up a main arterial road and I looked to the shadows knowing that to head to central London we needed to have them placed behind and slightly to the right (5 o'clock position) to be going in the right direction. We hit the Thames and turned right to leave the river on our left. When I thought we had gone far enough, and following a small group of bikers ahead of us we turned right and a couple of blocks later I felt we were somewhere in the region. I told Paul to ask a black cab driver to direct us to the halls, and amazingly we were in the block behind the venue, with all day parking meters there, and miraculously with a free spot to park in.

We assembled ourselves and walked around the block, joining the back of the queue for tickets. Agreeing to meet up at the van by four o'clock we all went our separate ways and picked out our own interests for the day. There were two halls which our tickets covered, and all the main motorcycle manufacturers were displaying their new models, trying to tempt us to put our names down for them. Some of the riders were supporting their team stands, selling early franchise clothing and boots. Leather jackets were being sold everywhere, waterproofs, if you could think of something you wanted, you would most likely find it there to buy. By the time we got back to the van the lads looked more like pack animals as they carried there booty back. Good job the van had room. We loaded up and chattered excitedly as we headed home. We stopped at the 24 hours café, the Red Lodge, for a fry up and leg stretch, getting home eventually about ten o'clock, in time for one at the local. Good day had by all. Paul unloaded the van at mine so that a couple of the lads could pick up their parts to take home, or to be put into the workshop for the various projects which were taking up my garage and workshop.

By now we had a few projects starting to be built in the workshop, most of the lads helping each other with practical assistance or mechanical know-how for those less able but equally willing to build something. For those not yet sure what they wanted to do the magazines were brought to the shed to be looked at. With most showing American choppers and bike festivals it started the brains whirring, inspiring the weird and whacky, or just genius machines. Anything could happen now, and it did, but the best part was seeing how the lads all helped each other to bring their ideas to fruition.

Alex spotted a 'trike' and decided to build one himself. There was only a couple of grainy photos in the magazine and no clarity of construction, but Alex was not just a good motorcycle mechanic, he was also into sports cars and had customised a Triumph GT6 – putting a 2.5 PI triumph engine in – remodeling the bonnet to house the slightly taller engine and inlet breather for the carbs – so had a lot of crossover skills to bring to his project. The funniest bit of his bonnet remodeling was when he initially sprayed it, the bulbous alteration was painted a dark red, and this made it look like a male organ. That was a source of amusement and quickly got changed.

Alex had a Honda 750cc which he wanted to use, so he stripped it down to its bare bones. He kept the frame more or less standard for ease of refitting the engine when ready, but cut off the rear end from the seating area backward. He was an engineer, and his father had a small engineering workshop which had a lot of useful industrial machinery and calibration devices, but better still, he was allowed free use of everything. With the now scavenged frame looking sorry for itself he rebuilt it, first by giving the yoke heat, he stretched it to give the rake he had decided it needed. The rear of the frame was given four frame extensions, welding a bit of pipe inside the frame, the extensions were set over the pipe and welded securely to house a T-frame section for the drive mechanisms. This was all shot blasted and the base was painted red ready to be rebuilt.

Looking through the magazines, Alex was unable to find any forks he liked, and those that were available were a bit expensive, so he bought some solid stainless steel hexagonal bar from his workplace, and using one of his father's machines, heated and twisted them. He then went ahead to build his own extended girder forks, fashioned loosely on the Vincent versions of the 1950s dream machines. He machined a couple of alloy blocks to make the slab yokes for the forks and fitted them to the front of the frame. He made risers to fit the handlebars which were a square framed T-section straight bars. The front end was completed with an eight spoke alloy wheel, and a pair of square stainless headlights which he mounted one over the other, double decker style.

The basic trike was born, having already sourced a couple of Lotus car wheels for the rear end. Tentatively being pieced together in the workshop, the next job was to make tank, seat, battery, oil tank and electrical gubbins areas. At first he wasn't sure how to approach making patterns for these essential sections. I was as ever in and out of the workshop, gleaning what snippets I could to store up for whenever I might need to know something. I knew just what to do. Going indoors I collected up a couple of cardboard boxes which had not yet been dumped. Scissors, pens, and sticky tape. Yes, I was a diligent Blue Peter viewer, and I knew about model making having spent hours as a child making farmyards, boats and all things considered fun at the time. Alex thought I had gone mad, until he realised that making cardboard mock ups of the tanks and boxes, once assembled taped and fitted, it was then an easy thing to cut and lay the item out flat for a pattern. With directions of folds scribbled onto the cardboard it showed where the metal versions needed to be bent and welded into shape. He was amazed when it proved to be the ideal way to go forward. No messy drawings to be misinterpreted, just build, copy and fit.

The seat was the next conundrum. It needed to be strong so Alex used his experience of fiberglass. We laid a film of foil over the area where the seat would go. At first not sure of how to build the back rest until I found an inner tube and pumped it three quarters full, bent it in two forming a half circle. again covered with foil as it was placed around the rear of the seat area. Alex then built this up with layers and layers of fiberglass, until if felt thick enough to be strong enough to lean on. He then put several more layers for safety and the seat base was formed. The fixing bolts secured through the base and frame, to be bolted tight from below. None of the base was to be visible so it did not need to be smooth, some firm seating foam was bought, plastic to waterproof the seat and leather for the final covering. How to fix it?

Looking around for ideas we decided to button it like a chesterfield sofa. A friend of mine was an upholsterer and I went to visit her, she showed me how to drape the leather over the seat, fold it into shape and stretch it from the middle outwards.. She even had a button covering machine so I could make my own buttons. Back to the workshop and the seat was sorted. The buttons used string threaded through from the top and tied through the fiberglass base, tied and then the final job was to fix the backing leather with glue. I must admit I was proud that I had been able to come up with a few ideas to make the trike viable.

The next bit was totally down to Alex's capability in mechanics. Not being able to just go out and buy a chain driven axle he set his mind to answers. With the access to various lathes and equipment he came up with making his own diff. He took the crown wheel of a Triumph 2000 to bits, made his own housing for it to sit in, incorporating a chain drive to fit the housing. He proceeded to fabricate and/or use appropriate parts to make a mini version of a Jaguar back end to form independent suspension to each rear wheel, with inboard discs rather than at the wheel end, and the back axle came into being. Alex fabricated stainless steel tie bars to triangulate the wheels back to the frame, mounted under the passenger footboards. The bike was longer than a standard bike, but that was sorted with working out the length of drive chain needed and ordering a bespoke chain. Stan was an ex-RAF electrical wizard and he helped make a wiring loom from scratch. Only thing left now was the paintwork. The tank was multi sided so the panels were taped and painted black with some ad hoc stars individually sprayed on the sides. The homemade rear wheel mudguards were painted in the same manner. The final touch was with the help of another friend. Nigel, was a great artist, and he made a silhouette outline of a dragon which was then used to spray the dragon directly onto the top panel of the tank. Once the outline was finished, the eyes and a few detailed markings were completed, the bike was now almost ready for going legal. A few trips to the library to make sure it complied with Construction and Use Regulations, a few adjustments, a DVLA inspection and we were good to go.

All this was done whilst mates around us were working on their own projects. Rodger was being a bit secretive of what he was building and although doing much of the work in our sheds, he assembled it all at home in a shed which was not much bigger than a broom cupboard. We used to laugh at his hiding himself under a bushel, but when he finally revealed his machine it was a beautiful work of art. He had made the tank himself, an intricate multi flat sided affair, the paint was stunning using a variety of paint finishes using candy, metallic and flip flop specialist paints. In Mid blue, pinks, gold, purple it was ahead of its time and just beautiful. The bike was a BSA with a small rake to the forks, but just simple in its construction. Just clean and gleaming, and a surprise to us all when he unveiled it for the summer.

Stan built his bike at the cottage, another Honda 750cc crash rebuild. As he was a long-distance lorry driver he did not have the same time to put into his bike, but with some off the shelf parts he did a fantastic job. He used a lot of the original donor bike, bought pattern parts and custom parts which made it unique to him. He wanted to be a bit extreme and bought a set of 18 inch over telescopic forks which he thought would be fun. They were. The final effort was painted white, with mirror flecks sprinkled all over, then lacquered with several layers on top. Again, simple but eye catching. He was rightly proud of his creation, especially in view of his limited timeframes. On the first trip on this creation, Stan had a minor hiccup. With the extended forks it took a bit of getting used to, and arriving at our local watering hole he miscalculated and hit the wall of the pub, having not made allowance for the length of the front end. He was riding slow enough to not damage anything, but it was a cursory lesson.

On the evenings when we went to the pub, talk was mostly about the various builds in progress. The lads at the farm workshop were in production, as were several mates in their own backyards and buildings. Rob had a BSA A10 plunger which he was grappling with. Although not there to see the progress of this bike, we heard about it during the pub updates. It was admired by his contemporaries and I was eager to see it. Most of the projects were being built ready for the spring and I would have to wait. When it was finally revealed I was impressed as it was created with a real flair, and as several of the boys had exchanged tips of where to get things, he had it painted in yellow, reds and golds, and if I remember rightly it had a fish scale effect etched in, making it another stand out build.

Obviously not all bikers are equal, and the hapless Dave had more ambition than capability. He was a few years younger than most of the lads and did not quite have the same acumen. He did join in the talk and would happily chat about his 'project', but unfortunately his parents were not of the bike friendly variety. He was not really allowed much access to tools and equipment, and wasn't yet part of the older groups. He did his best, but when he finally rode it down to show off his machine it looked a sorry state. I think he must have walked it up to the local park and done it in the car park. He had finished it with a Matt Black spray can, not too carefully, there were runs and flies stuck in the paintwork and it looked sad. The first 'Rat Bike' we had encountered. It amazed all of us that it ran at all.

So many friends had entered the building frenzy by then. One of the young girls became inspired and decided to get a bike of her own. She bought a dilapidated BSA C15 and together with her mate Tony set about cleaning it up, getting it working and 'on the road'. Janice was a pretty and happy young person, very scatter brained but enthusiastic, full of the joys of spring. With a limited budget she made do with what came to hand. She hand painted her bike with a pretty blue hammarite paint found in her father's shed, which turned out better than it sounds. However, she had problems getting it legal as she did not have a log book and did not have a registration plate on it. With her bike test looming quicker than the legalities, she improvised. She painted a metal plate black and painted a made up set of numbers on it. By the time she got the bike to the test station fifteen miles away, the examiner took one look at her bike and said, 'if you got that here unscathed, you have survived the road', and duly passed her the required certificate without any further ado. We all rolled around at her luck, anyone else would have been locked up. I can still picture her face, all smiles and dimples of pleasure.

Another of our mates who worked at sea decided to make himself a 'low-rider' chopper. He acquired a Triumph 650 which he customised at home during several of his home periods. He was another larger than life character, and amused us with his stories of mishaps and misfortune during the build. He did a fairly good job mechanically and we were all looking forward to seeing his project. Several of us were at the pub when he pulled up on this vision of beauty. 'Flash' was himself a tall man, over six feet tall, and in his build he had made the bike to his needs. Our sides hurt when we all went out to see his bike, we laughed so much. His 'low-rider' had turned out to be the tallest chopper we had ever seen and we nicknamed it the double decker. It suited Flash, but low it was not. The lowrider was in fact more of a high-rider.

With all this hive of activity there was always several bodies in the workshop, winter projects and productions alive and kicking, it was inevitable there would be the odd incident or two. Alex was normally quite careful but on one particular evening he was fully focused on a tricky part of a build. He needed a small bit of welding doing to a section of one of the brackets and for speed just put the item on the bench in the shed, got the welder out and proceeded to get to work. With mask on, focus on target, the sparks were flying. I walked in to see what was going on, to see that just beyond Alex the trash bin was alight and above it were all the cans of paints on a shelf. I tried to alert Alex but he didn't hear and was oblivious to cause and effect. Thankfully Rodger arrived on his motorbike, as he came in the door at the opposite end of the shed, he spotted the danger, still with his motorbike gloves on, with no more ado he calmly picked up the hot metal bin and walked it out into the garden, throwing it down on the pathway. My eyes put themselves back in their sockets and I was able to breathe again. Rodger walked back in as Alex raised his head, not realising he had nearly burned the wooden shed down.

By this time I was being overrun with tea and coffee mugs. A friend was selling a second hand dishwasher as she was having a fitted kitchen put in. I jumped at the chance and she showed me how to use it. A plumber friend came and fitted it in my kitchen. This made my life a bit easier as I got used to all the different compartments for tablets, liquids and salts needed for optimum operation. All was good, until I came home one day to find the kitchen unusually spotless, and smelling of soap. Even the floor had been washed. The boys were nowhere to be seen, and the pets seemed spooked. I went down the pub, where the boys were having a laugh, until they spotted me and went unusually quiet. Having worked out that something was amiss, they had to own up. There had been a lot of activity in the workshop and the kitchen was full of detritus. Deciding they had better wash up before I got home, they filled the dishwasher ready to set the cycle going. Having not watched the procedure, in their wisdom they thought, washing up liquid. But where does it go? They filled all the plastic compartments they could find, but with normal washing up liquid. Not only that but they did not think that was enough, so proceeded to squirt several large squeezes directly into the main wash area. Switching the start button on, they went back to the sheds to finish their projects for the day. One of them looked up and said it's snowing outside. What? It can't be, it's August! But looking out of the window all they could see was 'snow'. Looking a bit more carefully, the snow was travelling upwards. They rushed out to see what was going on, to find bubbles floating everywhere. Coming from the dog flap in the kitchen door. Racing to the kitchen, on opening the door there was an oozing of bubbles which fell out of the room around their feet. The bubbles were up and over the worktops in the kitchen, had overflown into the dining room and out of the dog flap into the garden where the breeze wafted them about. Apparently they all pitched in to try to get rid of the bubbles, resorting to a couple of wet towels to try to flatten the offending mess. They were relieved when I obviously saw the funny side of four grown men trying to dispose of a room and a half of relentless bubbles, which were defying them for ages until they finally got the upper hand and killed them. At least I got a cleaner than clean kitchen that week.

Another incident around this time was my fault. I had thought it would be nice to have some fresh rolls, so set about cooking a few 'part baked rolls' which were starting to appear in the supermarkets at that time, waiting for the hapless lesser able cooks to try out. I happily put them in the oven and went to see what was happening out in the sheds. While distracted in the workings outside, I promptly forgot about them. I finally went inside a couple of hours later to a burning smell emanating from the kitchen. It took a few seconds to remember the rolls. I turned the oven off, tried to save my offerings, but King Alfred would have been happy to know it was not all his fault. The buns were black. By black, I mean black, black, black. To the point that when Alex came into the kitchen behind me, he couldn't contain his amusement. Once they had cooled off he took them out to the workshop, drilled through five of them and mounted on a wire string gaily pronounced them as the workshop mascot. A warning to all not to eat at this table. The lads were equally wrapped up in the joke, and I had a lot to live down for the winter. At least I have always been able to laugh at myself.

It wasn't until we moved about eighteen months later that Alex took a hacksaw to one of the rolls, to find that not only were they black on the outside, they were black on the inside too, with less than 5mm of nearly white stuff in the centre. This joke was resurrected several times over the years.

Chapter 16 First Motorcycle Show at The Tavern

Several friends from slightly different geographical areas would pop in to the pub occasionally, so we heard about their offerings too. I guess it is a bit infectious in groups of friends, when one starts something then everyone likes to join in, and eventually there is a lot of activity. My friend John who lived on the coast was building a Harley Davidson. Barry had a Panther 600cc single which he was playing with. Steve was building a chopper in a nearby town about twelve miles away. Most of the lads I had hung around with before moving to my cottage had all been about standard bikes, but even some of them had played about – one of them had a Norvin, which was a Vincent in a Norton Frame, with 'Armageddon' written on the tank, in emulation of a bike in one of the regular comic strip features in a very popular magazine back then. Several of my former groups had built café racers too, with mixed names noting their changed heritage. Tritons, Tribsa, Norvins and Rickman variations to name just a few.

Several lads had built their customised machinery, for the time they were pretty formidable choppers. During their sessions in the workshop, many of the lads pored over the events and shows held in America and mourned the fact that there was nothing like that in Norfolk, and nor were we aware of any in the rest of England. A few bike magazines had 'Readers Rides' articles with photos showing the enthusiasm was out there, but they were not really accommodated for other than the larger MAG rallies and the annual BMF but they were as much for mainstream motorcycles rather than choppers and custom bikes. This did not hold the attention of the visionaries amongst our groups of mates. With talk down the pub of individuals doing their own builds, either in our workshop or their own garages and sheds, it seemed the bug had bitten. Taking my bike back for one of its services at Lowestoft, I was chatting to the mechanic there who I had now known for about four years. He was starting to build his own custom bikes, as well as some of his mates who were mechanically minded were also building their own visions of wonder. Seems like great minds are alike, and got me thinking.

The outcome of this was that one night, talk went around to many of the bikes being almost ready to be roadworthy. Tales of shows and events in America abounded, discussions about why is there nothing like that in our area, and disgruntled comments about the lack of somewhere to show off our various machinery. As usual my mouth opened and the idea of our own show came out. The lads all said, who could organise such a show, where could it be held? I held my hands up and said, that's not a problem, we can do it. There were moans about 'no experience', 'no funds' and other negative thoughts. A mate's wife came up to me and said she has organised loads of Scout Camps and Girl Guide events and would help me, she had a few contacts for acquiring cups and award plagues. Up I stood and said Helen and I will organise it, and so we did. We palled up, which was easy as she lived just up the road from me, on the same street.

We asked the landlord and landlady of our local pub if they would be willing to let us use the pub as the venue. There was a reasonable amount of car parking and we could use the pub's car park as the show area. They made a good living out of us bikers and with the eye on the profit, they thought double or triple that customer base would be welcome; the following weekend we put a bucket on the bar and with a sign on it which announced the show date and welcomed donations towards prizes which would be greatly appreciated. We settled on a date early summer, we chose a Sunday as the roads would be quiet and the local businesses were shut, and we were free to set it up.

Helen and I enjoyed working out what we would do, and came up with the idea of several distinctive groups. There could be a 'Best British' 'Best Jap' 'Best European' 'Best Chopper' 'Best Rat' 'Best of Show' and 'Landlord's Choice'. seven categories seemed ambitious but we thought it was fairer, and the landlord enjoyed having his own choice to award. We used raffle tickets and charged £1 for six tickets for show goers to vote for their favourite bikes, with boxes for each of the categories voted on. We bought trophies and a couple of plaques and we were ready for the day. The proceeds were to go to a local charity. We covered what we thought would be fun for everyone. We designed and had some flyers printed and distributed them to as many bike shops we could think of, passing some to friends to put in their areas as well.

When the show day came around, the lads all met at the pub at 10am, they helped rope the pub car park off, we used Helen's Bedford Van to display the 'prizes' and cups. Helen borrowed the loudspeaker from her Scouts Club. We weren't sure what sort of turnout it would be, but were happy enough to know we would have a bit of fun whatever. We were astounded by the response. Bikes started turning up early around 11am despite the posters timing from noon to 6pm. Bikes continued turning up from then on. The pub was packed to the brim, having to beg steal and borrow kegs from other pubs in the area. The bikes were parked along the road, in every nearby bit of concrete, tarmac or gravel which had space for another bike. There was no room unoccupied for about a half mile radius. There was so much commotion as bikes and cars turned up in droves. People would see something going on and stop to come and have a look. The show had been a success, our town was on the map for bikers, and it was amazing to see how many people turned up. The buzz was exhilarating as friends caught up with mates who had drifted from their areas as they came from all over the county in response to the posters put up in and around Norfolk.

The outcome from our show left us to repeat it, and our custom show ran for 10 consecutive years. We were not a club, just a load of friends with an idea for a bit of fun. Most of those original group still met regularly over the next five decades. It just goes to show that friendships forged from similar interests can stand the test of time. I was privileged to have been part of this branch of kinship. Helen is still one of the best people I know, 50 years on and like myself still riding and partying. Who needs a Zimmer frame when a pair of handlebars are close to hand, and closer still to the heart.

PS, it only took me 38 years to get my first book (Manners, Morals and Motorbikes) out into the wide world. This sequel was quick, (Trials, Triumphs and Travelling) only 3 years and then possibly the next (Men, Marriage and Mayhem) will positively bounce off the pages.

Thank you to those who have left reviews so far, I am encouraged.

I intend to write about the incidents and funny events in my life, without any character assassinations. Again, I want to inspire love and laughter and reminiscences which are bound to be similar to many people of the era. So please, feel free to join me on my further adventures.

Don't miss out!

Visit the website below and you can sign up to receive emails whenever CJ McLeod publishes a new book. There's no charge and no obligation.

https://books2read.com/r/B-A-JEYAB-FQPPC

BOOKS 2 READ

Connecting independent readers to independent writers.

Also by CJ McLeod

Motorcycle Chronicals
Manners, Morals & Motorbikes
Trials, Triumphs and Travelling

About the Author

Born and raised in Brighton, lived in Denmark and Tenerife before returning to live in Norfolk in 1972, my childhood was unusual to say the least.

There was a 42 year gap between my parents who met during their stage careers, father being the show owner, mother one of the dancers - their relationship was temptestuous. My father was the better carer of the two - even though he was 67 when he fathered me - but I remember him doing his best to look after myself and my two sisters. He taught me to be confident and to stand up for myself.

I was six when my parents split up, by the time I was 16 had moved house 18 times, moved country 4 times and attended 14 different schools in three countries. I initially left school at the age of 14 to work for a wood carver on the local market, but when arriving back in the UK I had to go back to school and be a child again.

With the genetic makeup of an East End Londoner mixed with a Texan cowboy of Scottish/Mexican ancestry, meant,

I could never be 'normal'.